Practical English

for Junior College Students

우종현

우종현(Jonghyeon Woo)

○ 영문학 박사
○ 백석문화대학교 교수
○ 한국영어어문교육학회 이사(전)
○ 한국현대영어학회 이사(전)

Practical English
for Junior College Students

© 우종현, 2018
1판 1쇄 인쇄__2018년 08월 10일
1판 1쇄 발행__2018년 08월 20일
지은이__우종현
펴낸이__이종엽
펴낸곳__글모아출판
        등록__제324-2005-42호
공급처__(주)글로벌콘텐츠출판그룹
        대표__홍정표 이사__양정섭
        편집디자인__김미미 기획·마케팅__노경민 이종훈
        주소__서울특별시 강동구 풍성로 87-6 201호
        전화__02) 488-3280 팩스__02) 488-3281
        홈페이지__http://www.gcbook.co.kr
값 13,000원
ISBN 978-89-94626-75-8 93740

Practical English

for Junior College Students

우종현 지음

글모아출판

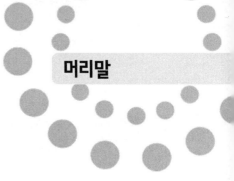

이 책은 초급대학 학생들이 기본적으로 알아야 할 영어 습득 학습서로서 특히 교실수업 활용을 위해 엮어졌다.

한 학기 15주 강의를 위해 전체 내용을 15개 Lesson으로 구분하였으며, 각 Lesson은 Topic based vocabulary & conversation, short question & answer 그리고 Grammar study로 2~3시간 교실 수업내용으로 구성되어 있다.

일상생활에서 기본적으로 알아야 할 단어를 주제별로 짧은 대화와 함께 제시하고, 영문법에서 제시하고 있는 모든 영역을 쉽고 단순하게 설명함으로써 학습자들이 편안하게 접근할 수 있도록 하였다.

contents

contents

Exercise Actions

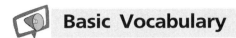

stretch	bend
walk	run
hop	jump
kneel	lie down
swing	push
pull	lift
push-up	handstand
throw	kick
sit-up	pull-up
skip	somersault

Are there any sport centers around here?

Linda: Are there any sport centers around here?

Andrew: Yes. There is a sport center named 24 Hours next to the Wal-Mart.

Linda: Oh, really! I think it is a famous sport center in USA.

Andrew: Yes it is. I go to the center after work. I usually do walk and run. I can do 30 push-ups at one time.

Linda: Wow, great! I can't believe it.
I want to buy the membership card. I would like to do pull-ups everyday.

Andrew: That's good for you. I can ride you to the center.

Now _____ like this.

A: Let's do twenty _____.

B: Twenty _____ are too heavy for me.

A: Which exercise do you do?

B: I do _____ and _____ everyday.

1. When did you finish the project?

2. What does your father do for a living?

3. How was the weather?

4. Are there any messages for me?

5. I'd like extra prints of this photograph.

6. May I ask a question?

7. Do you have any bags to check?

8. Can I give you a piece of advice?

9. May I ask a favor of you?

10. Why don't we take a break?

1. When did you finish the project?

   (A) The project is very important.

   (B) Tomorrow is fine for me.

   (C) I did it yesterday.

2. What does your father do for a living?

   (A) He lives in Seoul.

   (B) He can do anything he likes.

   (C) He is a programmer.

3. How was the weather?

   (A) They were wet together.

   (B) It was very cold.

   (C) It will be fine tomorrow.

4. Are there any messages for me?

   (A) You can leave messages.

   (B) Your sister called at 3 o'clock.

   (C) The massage room is at the end of the hall.

5. I'd like extra prints of this photograph.

   (A) I'm sorry but the fax isn't working.

   (B) No problem.

   (C) This printer is not for sale.

6. May I ask a question?

    (A) You may go home.

    (B) Sure, What's it?

    (C) It's a good question.

7. Do you have any bags to check?

    (A) The bag is mine.

    (B) I'll be back tomorrow.

    (C) No, I'll carry my suitcase.

8. Can I give you a piece of advice?

    (A) I can take a piece of pie.

    (B) Thank you. I'm listening.

    (C) No thanks. I'm full.

9. May I ask a favor of you?

    (A) Why don't you ask me?

    (B) Sure. What can I do for you?

    (C) Yes. It's one of my favorite books.

10. Why don't we take a break?

    (A) It will take 30 minutes.

    (B) You can take the bus.

    (C) That's a good idea.

문장의 구조(Sentence Structure)

> 의미: 다른 나라 언어와 마찬가지로, 영어 문장이 되기 위해서는 일정한 구조
> 적인 규칙을 가지고 있으며, 이 규칙에 따라 문장을 사용할 때 비로써
> 의미를 확정한다.

1. 문장의 구성요소 및 성분

1) 문장의 구성 요소: 단어, 구, 절

단어: 말의 최소 단위로서 영어에서는 그 특성(품사)에 따라 8가지로 구분

I love peace.

구(Phrase): 두 개 이상의 단어가 한 덩어리가 되어 의미를 갖는 것

My mother takes care of many children.

절(Clause): 두 개 이상의 단어가 한 덩어리가 되어 의미를 가지면서, 주어와
동사(술어)관계가 있는 것

I think the boy is honest.

* 단어의 특성(품사)
  : 모든 단어는 8가지 특성으로 구분되며, 이것을 "품사"라고 한다.

명사: 사람, 사물 등 유·무형을 지칭
예) book, family, love, water, Seoul

대명사: 명사를 대신해서 받는 것

   예) I, you, he, she, they, we, it

동사: 동작이나 상태를 나타내는 것

   예) go, come, run, study, see, eat

형용사: 명사의 성질이나 상태를 나타냄

   예) beautiful, good, kind, happy, honest

부사: 여러 다른 품사의 상태를 나타내고, 장소, 방법, 시간, 이유 등을 표현

   예) very, pretty, easily, fast, happily

접속사: 단어와 단어, 구와 구, 절과 절 등을 연결

   예) and, or, but, that, because

전치사: 명사를 목적어로 해서 기본 문장을 확장

   예) in, at, on, from, for

감탄사: 놀람이나 감탄을 나타낸다.

   예) wow, oh

2) 문장 성분: 문장에서 어떤 쓰임을 하느냐에 따라 주어, 술어(동사), 목적어, 보어 등으로 구분하는데 이를 문장 성분이라 한다.

주어: 문장의 주체로서 '은/는/이/가'로 해석

동사(술어): 문장을 서술해 주는 것으로서 '~다'로 해석

보어: 주어나 목적어를 설명하는 것

목적어: 주어 행위의 대상으로서 '~에게' 또는 '을/를'로 해석

I painted the door green.

   (I: 주어, painted: 동사, the door: 목적어, green: 보어)

2. 문장의 기본 구조(문장의 5가지 형태)

모든 영어 문장은 5가지 구조를 가지고 있는데, 이것을 문장의 5형식이라고 하며 1형식문장, 2형식문장, 3형식문장, 4형식문장, 5형식문장이라고 각각 말해진다.

1) 1형식: 주어 + 동사(Subject + Verb)

The sun rises.
Birds sing.
My father works.

2) 2형식: 주어 + 동사 + 보어(S + V + Complement)

I am happy.
He became a doctor.
She looks happy.
She appears sensible.

* 대표적인 2형식 동사
be, become, go, grow, get, look, appear, seem, remain

3) 3형식: 주어 + 동사 + 목적어(S + V + Object)

I like apples.
I met him.
They helped the man.
I finished the project.

4) 4형식: 주어 + 동사 + 간접목적어 + 직접목적어
(S + V + O + Indirect Object + Direct Object)

I gave her the book.
  → I gave the book to her. (3형식)
He sent the patient flowers.
  → He sent flowers to the patient. (3형식)
Linda teaches us English.
  → Linda teaches English to us. (3형식)

* 4형식을 3형식으로 고칠 때 to를 사용하지 않는 동사
  buy, build, make, get, order, cook, receive: for + I.O.
    I'll make some coffee for you.

  ask, require, beg, demand, inquire: of + I.O.
    He asked a question of me.

  play, impose, confer: on + I.O.
    He played a trick on me.
    They imposed a tax of 100 dollars on me.

5) 5형식: 주어 + 동사 + 목적어 + 보어(S + V + O + C)

We elected him president.
I found this book easy.
I painted the desk blue.
They believed the boy honest.

3. 동사의 종류

동사를 분류하는 데는 다양한 방법이 있는데, 문장을 만들 때는 동사(술어)가 그 다음에 오는 문장 성분을 선택하게 된다. 따라서 문장을 만들 때에는 동사의 선택이 중요하며, 동사의 선택에 따라 문장이 구분되어 만들어진다.

자동사: 목적어를 선택하지 않는 동사

The earth <u>moves</u>. (1형식)

She <u>became</u> a singer. (2형식)

타동사: 목적어를 선택하는 동사

I don't <u>know</u> the doctor. (3형식)

The boy <u>sent</u> the girl a present. (4형식)

We <u>called</u> him a fool. (5형식)

Exercise

A. 밑줄 친 단어의 품사를 구분하세요.

1. I forgot to book a <u>ticket</u> for the movie.
2. I am going to meet him <u>at</u> the coffee shop.
3. Mary <u>and</u> Tom look very happy.
4. He showed her an <u>expensive</u> computer.
5. English is not <u>so</u> easy for me.
6. The man invited <u>my</u> sister yesterday.

B. 아래 문장에서 밑줄 친 동사를 자동사와 타동사로 구분하세요.

1. He <u>smiles</u> at me.
2. We <u>made</u> a reservation.
3. They <u>went</u> to the park in the morning.
4. I <u>found</u> the book difficult.
5. They don't <u>want</u> to take a bus.

C. 아래 문장이 몇 형식 문장인지 구분하세요.

1. The beautiful bird is singing on the tree.
2. I thought it a dog.
3. The man killed himself on Monday.
4. Seoul is the capital of Korea.
5. Could you lend me your pen?

Occupations

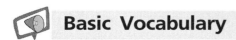

teacher	professor
lawyer	scientist
doctor	nurse
pharmacist	pilot
police officer	secretary
architect	carpenter
mechanic	photographer
painter	cook/chef
security guard	fire fighter
model	hairdresser

What do you do?

Jordan: How do you do? I am Jordan.

Logan: How do you do? My name is Logan.

Jordan: What do you do?

Logan: I am a chef. I work for a Korean Restaurant at downtown.

Jordan: Really! I like Korean food. How long have you worked for the restaurant.

Logan: I have worked for the restaurant since last year. What's your occupation?

Jordan: I am a lawyer, but I wanted to be a teacher.

Logan: Are you satisfied with your job?

Jordan: Yes, I am.

I'd like to be a(n) _____.

My _____ is a _____.

A: What's your occupation?!

B: I am a(an) _____.

A: Are you still a(n) _____?

B: No, I am a(n) _____.

1. Where do you like to go for your vacation?

2. Who is coming with you?

3. Why don't you have lunch with me?

4. Are you ready to order?

5. Officer, someone just stole my bag!

6. Mr. Brown is supposed to visit tonight, isn't he?

7. Do you drive to work?

8. Could you tell me your office hours?

9. May I speak with John?

10. Can you be back before lunch?

Choosing the correct answer.

1. Where do you like to go for your vacation?

   (A) I already had my vacation.

   (B) A ski resort is best for me.

   (C) I am going there with my son.

2. Who is coming with you?

   (A) My brother wants to.

   (B) It's very cunning.

   (C) I am coming now.

3. Why don't you have lunch with me?

   (A) I am sorry. I've already had lunch.

   (B) There are many people in the restaurant.

   (C) I don't have an umbrella.

4. Are you ready to order?

   (A) Yes, I want to play with you.

   (B) Yes, I am ready to go.

   (C) Can I have ice cream?

5. Officer, someone just stole my bag!

   (A) Calm down, and tell me exactly what happened.

   (B) Who are you calling a thief?

   (C) OK, I'll give the bag back to him.

6. Mr. Brown is supposed to visit tonight, isn't he?

    (A) Yes, he is in the office.

    (B) Yes, tonight will be fine.

    (C) Yes, he called earlier to confirm his visit.

7. Do you drive to work?

    (A) No, I take the subway.

    (B) Yes, I have to work.

    (C) Yes, I worked all day.

8. Could you tell me your office hours?

    (A) I get up at 6:00.

    (B) Don't tell a lie.

    (C) From nine to eleven.

9. May I speak with John?

    (A) You can speak with anybody.

    (B) I'm sorry. he's out.

    (C) He wants to see.

10. Can you be back before lunch?

    (A) I have already a big bag.

    (B) I am not sure, but I'll try.

    (C) I had lunch with him.

문장의 종류(Types of sentence)

의미: 의사표현을 하는 데 있어, 말을 하는 사람이 상대방에게 어떤 사실이나, 상태를 자신의 의도에 따라 구분해서 문장을 선택하며, 4가지로 구분된다.

평서문: 어떤 사실이나 상태를 평범하게 나타내는 문장

의문문: 어떤 사실이나 상태에 대해 의견 또는 대답을 요구하는 문장

명령문: 말하는 이가 자신 또는 듣는 사람에게 무엇을 시키거나 행동을 요구하는 문장

감탄문: 자신의 감정이나 느낌을 강하게 표현하는 문장

*긍정문과 부정문: 위 문장들을 때로는 긍정문으로, 때로는 부정문으로 표현된다.

1. 평서문: 주어 + 동사의 어순으로 쓴다.

The lion runs very fast.

I am very happy.

Billy loved Jane at that time.

She bought him a bicycle.

They made her sad.

He can speak English very well.

§ 평서문의 부정문 만들기

1) be동사가 있는 평서문: be동사 뒤에 not을 붙인다.

He is a doctor.

→ He is not a doctor.

The cat is dangerous.

→ The cat is not dangerous.

2) 조동사가 있는 평서문: 조동사 뒤에 not을 붙인다.

He can speak English.

→ He can't speak English.

We will meet the mayor at the city hall.

→ We will not meet the mayor at the city hall.

3) 일반동사가 있는 평서문: 'do'동사를 일반동사 앞에 넣고 do동사 다음에 not을 붙인다.

I want to study with him.

→ I don't want to study with him.

Linda loves John.

→ Linda does not love John.

They made her sad.

→ They did not make her sad.

2. 의문문: 의문사 있는 의문문과 의문사 없는 의문문으로 구분되며, 동사 + 주어의 어순을 갖는다.

1) 의문사 없는 의문문: 주어와 동사의 어순이 동사 + 주어의 순서가 된다.

(1) be동사가 있는 평서문: be동사가 문장 앞으로 간다.

She is a famous singer.

→ Is she a famous singer?

They are angry.

→ Are they angry?

(2) 조동사가 있는 평서문: 조동사가 문장 앞으로 간다.

They can play the piano.

→ Can they play the piano.

He will write a novel.

→ Will he write a novel.

(3) 일반동사가 있는 평서문: 'do'동사를 문장 앞에 넣고, 원래 있던 동사는 '원형'을 사용한다.

I met the woman.

→ Did I meet her?

She teaches him English.

→ Does she teach him English?

They elected the man mayor.

→ Did they elect the man mayor?

2) 의문사 있는 의문문: When, Where, Who, What, How, Why 등의 의문사가 있
는 의문문으로서, 의문사는 항상 문두에 위치하며, 동사 + 주어
의 어순을 유지한다.

When do you want to go there?

Where is the police station?

Who is the man over there?

What shall I do next time?

How can I help you?

Why are they so excited?

3. 명령문: 명령뿐만 아니라 청유, 정중한 부탁(간접명령)도 포함되며, 일반적으로
상대방에게 지시하는 것이기 때문에 주어 'You'가 생략되어 동사원형
으로 시작된다.

Do it yourself.

Open the door, please.

Let me introduce myself.

Let me say.

* 명령문 다음에 오는 'and'는 '그러면'으로 'or'는 '그러지 않으면'으로 해석

Study hard, and you will pass the test.

Work hard, or you will be fired.

4. 감탄문: 평서문을 사용해서 감탄을 나타내기도 하고, 'how'나 'what'을 사용해서 감탄을 표현한다.

You are so beautiful!

What a nice day it is!
  (What a/an 명사 주어 동사)

How pretty it is!
  (How 형용사 주어 동사)

A. 아래 문장의 종류를 구분하세요.

평서문, 의문문, 명령문, 감탄문

1. What a kind man he is!
2. Did you meet him yesterday?
3. Let him go.
4. Is she a teacher?
5. The program is very useful.

B. 아래 문장들을 부정문으로 만드세요.

1. My uncle was very diligent.
2. My sister watched the TV show yesterday.
3. They paint the roof white.
4. William sent Linda the jewelry box.
5. I can do it.

C. 아래 문장들을 의문문으로 만드세요.

1. He is interested in politics.
2. Susan is from America.
3. She likes to talk on the phone.
4. Birds sing in the forest.
5. She will do her best tomorrow.

Describing People

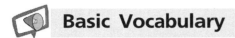

happy	frustrated
nervous	sad
miserable	upset
jealous	proud
angry	crazy/mad
confused	disappointed
surprised	afraid
scared	satisfied
shocked	embarrassed
annoyed	shameful

How are you doing?

Linda: How are you today, Andrew?
You look angry.

Andrew: I am just in a bad mood.

Linda: Why? Are you upset about something?

Andrew: Yeah, My car wouldn't start this morning.
It was driving me crazy.

Linda: What did you do?

Andrew: I took a taxi. So, I was late at the meeting.
There were many people waiting for me.

Linda: How about taking a break?

Andrew: Okay, This has been a long day.

Linda: See you tomorrow!

Andrew: Take care.

He is very _____.

He is _____ than me

A: Are you _____?

B: Yes, I am _____.

A: What makes you _____.

B: _____ makes me _____.

A: When do you feel _____.

B: I am _____ when I feel _____.

1. Where would you like to visit?

2. What are you going to do after school?

3. How do you usually get to school?

4. Is smoking allowed in this shop?

5. Something smells delicious!

6. This is your first day in the office, isn't it?

7. Do you have the time?

8. Can we check the inventory now?

9. May I speak to Wilson?

10. What are you going to do?

Choosing the correct answer

1. Where would you like to visit?

   (A) I live in Seoul.

   (B) I visited Seoul yesterday.

   (C) I want to see the stock market.

2. What are you going to do after school?

   (A) I have to read my book.

   (B) I will go fishing tomorrow.

   (C) we go to school.

3. How do you usually get to school?

   (A) I'm fine.

   (B) I'm going to school.

   (C) On foot.

4. Is smoking allowed in this shop?

   (A) No it isn't. Care for a cigarette?

   (B) Yes, but only in smoking seats.

   (C) I'm thinking about it.

5. Something smells delicious!

   (A) It's beef pie.

   (B) It's a new fragrance by Chanel.

   (C) Yes, I'll try my best.

6. This is your first day in the office, isn't it?

   (A) Yes, I'll miss you a lot.

   (B) Yes, it is. I'm so excited.

   (C) Yes, today's my birthday.

7. Do you have the time?

   (A) I am sorry. I have enough time.

   (B) Time can not wait.

   (C) Five o'clock sharp.

8. Can we check the inventory now?

   (A) I'm sorry. I don't have a check.

   (B) Sure. Let's do it.

   (C) You have to check the tire.

9. May I speak to Wilson?

   (A) Yes, you can leave a message.

   (B) I am sorry. He is out.

   (C) He is the manager of the Wilson market.

10. What are you going to do?

    (A) I have many plants.

    (B) I really want to go abroad.

    (C) I will take the bag with me.

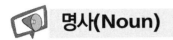 **명사(Noun)**

의미: 사람, 사물, 유·무형을 말하는 단어

역할: 문장에서 주어, 목적어, 보어 역할

▽ 명사의 종류

셀 수 있는 명사: 문장에서 단수, 복수 구분을 해야 한다.

　　　　　　　　보통명사, 집합명사

셀 수 없는 명사: 단수 취급을 하며, 복수형을 만들 수 없다.

　　　　　　　　물질명사, 추상명사, 고유명사

1. 보통명사: 같은 종류의 사람, 사물, 동물에 공통적으로 붙일 수 있는 명사

예) book, pen, desk, house, room, door, window, board, projector

I read a book.

He likes apples.

2. 집합명사: 사람, 또는 사물의 집합체를 나타내는 명사

1) 집합체의 단일성을 강조하면 단수취급

2) 집합체의 개별성을 강조하면 복수취급

예) family, public, audience, team, committee, faculty

His family is very large.
His family get up all early in the morning.
The committee meets once a week.
The committee express their opinions at the meeting.

3. 물질명사: 일정한 모양을 갖추지 않은 물질을 나타내는 명사

예) water, tea, coffee, paper, old, oil, milk, sugar, salt, money, sand

Milk is made into butter and cheese.
This box was made of paper.

* 물질명사의 수량 표시
  a glass of water,   two glasses of water
  a sheet of paper,   three sheets of paper
  a bottle of beer,   two bottles of beer
  a cup of coffee,   two cups of coffee
  a pound of sugar,   two pounds of sugar

4. 추상명사: 눈으로 볼 수도 없고 손으로 만질 수도 없는 추상적인 무형의 명사. 원칙적으로 관사를 사용할 수 없으며, 복수형도 되지 않는다.

예) art, beauty, wisdom, truth, love, honesty, peace, news, youth, time, success, failure

Life is short and art is long.
The man was wild in his youth.

* 추상명사의 수량 표시
a piece of information
a piece of news
a piece of advice

5. 고유명사: 특정한 사람, 사물, 장소, 회사에 쓰이는 고유한 이름 나타내는 명사

Hanlasan is the highest mountain in Korea.
Shakespeare is an excellent writer.
Samsung is a big company.

▽ 명사의 수

셀 수 있는 명사(보통명사, 집합명사)는 문장에서 사용될 때, 단수인지 복수인지를 확인하여 사용해야 한다. 단, 셀 수 없는 명사는 원칙적으로 단수로만 사용된다.

▽ 명사의 복수형 만들기

1. 규칙변화

1) 대부분의 단어 끝에 -s를 붙인다.

예) books, doctors, students, pens, apples, tigers, lions, sons, flowers

2) 어미가 -s, -ss, -x, -sh, -ch로 끝나면 -es를 붙인다.

예) buses, glasses, boxes, dishes, benches, peaches, brushes

3) 자음 + y로 끝나는 단어는 y를 i로 고친 뒤 -es를 붙인다.

예) ladies, cities, babies, soliloquies, duties, flies

4) 「자음 + o」는 -es를 붙인다.

예) potatoes, heroes, negroes, echoes

* 주의: 「자음 + o」라도 -s만 붙이는 경우가 있다.
  예) pianos, solos, autos, photos, memos, sopranos

5) 어미가 -f(e)로 끝나면 -f를 -ves로 고친다.

예) lives, thieves, knives, leaves, wives, wolves, shelves
* 주의: roofs, chiefs, safes, cliffs, proofs

2. 불규칙변화

1) 모음을 변화시켜 복수로 만드는 경우

　예) men, feet, women, geese, teeth, mice

2) -en, -ren을 붙여 복수로 만드는 경우

　예) children, oxen

3) 단수와 복수의 형태가 같은 단어

　예) sheep, deer, salmon, trout, fish

A. 아래 문장에서 명사에 밑줄을 치고, 그 종류(보통, 집합, 물질, 추상, 고유)를 쓰세요.

1. The boy wants to be a good doctor.
2. He ordered a cup of coffee.
3. The audience have to pay extra money for the concert.
4. There are many people in Seoul.
5. Honesty is very important.

B. 아래 문장에서 밑줄 친 명사가 셀 수 있는 명사인지(가산), 아닌지(불가산)를 표시하세요.

1. There are many churches in the city.
2. He is a smart student.
3. Jane loves Tom.
4. She went to the Busan.
5. We paid much money.
6. Glass is easy to break.
7. We had much snow last winter.
8. The traveller wanted some water.
9. The team won the game.
10. Knowledge is very important.

Exercise

C. 아래 문장에서 밑줄 친 부분을 바르게 고치세요. 필요하면 a/an을 첨가하세요.

1. There are many <u>potato</u> in the shop.
2. Could you lend me <u>car</u>?
3. I don't understand <u>a English</u>.
4. He come from <u>a Japan</u>.
5. <u>A milk</u> is good for health.
6. The roof is covered with <u>a snow</u>.
7. There are three <u>knife</u> on the table.
8. They took care of three <u>baby</u>.

Physical States

tired	sleepy
exhausted	hungry
thirsty	sick/ill
headache	toothache
stomachache	fever
cold	cough
infection	sunburn
chills	dizzy
earache	rash
sore throat	runny nose

What are your symptoms?

Linda: You look tired, Andrew?

Andrew: I think I just have a cold. I didn't sleep well last three days because I had to finish my project until this morning.

Linda: What are your symptoms?

Andrew: I have a fever, sore throat and runny nose.

Linda: Did you take any medicine?

Andrew: No I didn't. I am going to see a doctor after work.

Linda: I think you had better hurry up. Take lots of rest and feel better soon.

Andrew: Thanks.

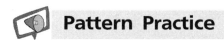

You look _____.

I have _____.

A: What's your symptoms?

B: I have _____ and _____.

A: When do you feel _____.

B: I am _____ when I am _____.

1. Where did you have lunch?

2. Who's in charge?

3. How is the weather?

4. Are you a vegetarian?

5. These cookies are tasty! Try one!

6. Rents for offices are really high around here, aren't they?

7. Do you mind if I visit you tomorrow?

8. Could you ask him to proofread the article?

9. May I help you?

10. Can I take my room key?

Choosing the correct answer

1. Where did you have lunch?

   (A) I don't have any plan.

   (B) I haven't had it yet.

   (C) I love to eat meat.

2. Who's in charge?

   (A) They charged 20 dollars.

   (B) I don't know how to charge.

   (C) Mr. Gates.

3. How is the weather?

   (A) It's very interesting.

   (B) It's cold.

   (C) I'm fine.

4. Are you a vegetarian?

   (A) Yes, I don't like meat.

   (B) There are many vegetables in the yard.

   (C) Yes, I am Hungarian.

5. These cookies are tasty! Try one!

   (A) They've already been tested by our team.

   (B) What's in them?

   (C) But I'm allergic to peach.

6. Rents for offices are really high around here, aren't they?

(A) Right. That's why we're planning to move.

(B) Yes, this area is the cheapest in this city.

(C) Yes, the office is on the 30th floor.

7. Do you mind if I visit you tomorrow?

(A) No, I'd love to see you.

(B) It will be fine tomorrow.

(C) Yes, you can do that.

8. Could you ask him to proofread the article?

(A) Sure, I'll ask him.

(B) Sure, I'll prove my innocence.

(C) No problem. I can read the book.

9. May I help you?

(A) What can I do for you?

(B) Yes, give me a hand.

(C) Yes, I can.

10. Can I take my room key?

(A) Yes, here you are.

(B) Yes, you take the newspaper.

(C) Sure, you have to lock the door.

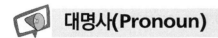 **대명사(Pronoun)**

의미: 명사를 대신해서 받는 단어

역할: 문장에서 주어, 목적어, 보어 역할을 한다.

▽ 대명사의 종류: 인칭대명사, 지시대명사, 부정대명사

§ 인칭대명사

인칭		주격	소유격	목적격	소유대명사	재귀대명사
1인칭	단수	I	my	me	mine	myself
	복수	we	our	us	ours	ourselves
2인칭	단수	you	your	you	yours	yourself
	복수	you	your	you	yours	yourselves
3인칭	단수	he	his	him	his	himself
		she	her	her	hers	herself
		it	its	it		itself
	복수	they	their	them	theirs	themselves

1. we, you, they가 일반인을 나타내는 경우가 있다. 이 때 we, you, they는 해석하지 않는 것이 자연스럽다.

We should keep our promise.

They say that he is honest.

You should not speak ill of others.

2. 소유대명사

소유격 + 명사 = 소유대명사

Your cell phone is new, but mine is old.

3. 재귀대명사

1) 강조 용법: 강조나 대조를 나타내기 위해 명사나 대명사 뒤에 쓰이며, 생략하여도 문법상으로 지장이 없고, 강조하는 말 뒤나 문미에 위치한다.

I myself carried the suitcase.
He did it himself.

2) 재귀적 용법: 문장의 목적어가 주어와 동일인[사물]인 경우에 쓰인다.

He killed himself.
History repeats itself.

3) 관용적 용법

He did it for himself. (혼자 힘으로)
He went there by himself. (혼자서)
The door opened of itself. (저절로)

4. It의 용법

1) 앞에 나온 어구(명사, 구, 절)를 받는다.

I tried to open the box, but it was impossible.

2) 비 인칭대명사 it: 특별히 가리키는 것이 없이, 문장을 만들기 위해서 주어 자리에 쓰는 것을 말한다. 이 때 it은 시간, 계절, 날씨, 거리, 명암을 나타낸다.

What time is it now? (시간)
It is spring now. (계절)
It is fine today. (날씨)
How long does it take from here to the station? (거리)
It is dark in the room. (명암)

§ 지시대명사

this/these, that/those

1) 가까운 것/먼 것

This is a pen.
That is a book.

2) 전자/후자(that/this)

He keeps one dog and one cat; this is more faithful than that.

3) 명사의 반복을 피하기 위한 that/those.

The tail of a fox is longer than that of a cat.

§ 부정대명사

1. one의 용법

1) 일반적인 사람을 나타낸다. 이 때 one은 해석되지 않는다.

One should keep one's promise.
One should obey one's parents.

2) 앞에 나온 명사의 반복을 피하기 위해서 쓴다.
a + 단수보통명사: one(같은 종류의 다른 물건)
the/this/that + 단수보통명사: it(똑같은 바로 그 물건)

If you need a book. I will lend you one.
I bought that book, but I lost it.

2. some과 any의 용법
some은 긍정문에서, any는 의문문, 부정문, 조건문에 쓰인다.

Some of the employees work really hard.

He asked for some money, but I didn't give him any.

If you need any money, I'll lend some to you.

3. all, both, every, each

1) all은 가산명사와 쓰일 때는 복수 취급, 불가산명사와 쓰일 때는 단수 취급한다.

All of them were happy.

All the money was spent.

All were happy.

2) 부분부정: every, all, both가 부정어와 같이 쓰이면 부분부정이 된다.

He didn't eat all of the tangerines.

I did not invite all of them.

Every bird can not sing.

They don't know everything.

Both of them did not come.

I do not know both of them.

A. 괄호 안에 알맞은 인칭대명사를 써 넣으세요.

1. This question is very difficult for (   ).
2. This pen is (   ).
3. She sent (   ) a letter.
4. (   ) work for Samsung.
5. The man asked me (   ) address.

B. 괄호 안에 알맞은 대명사를 써 넣으세요.

1. The girl showed me a red sweater, but I don't like (   ).
2. This dog is stronger than (   ).
3. They were proud of (   ) for winning the game.
4. He said the bag was (   ).
5. My mother bought me blue neck ties, and I really like
   (   ).
6. If you need a pen, I will give (   ) to you.

C. 아래 문장에서 밑줄 친 'it'의 쓰임을 구분하세요.

1. <u>It</u> is snowing outside.
2. How far is <u>it</u> from here to the mall.
3. Tom bought a car and he drove <u>it</u> to the school.
4. How far is <u>it</u> from here to the mall.
5. I tried to open the box, but <u>it</u> was impossible.
6. <u>It</u> is already five.

Describing Body

head	hair
forehead	eyebrow
eye	ear
nose	cheek
mouth	jaw
lip	tooth/teeth
tongue	neck
shoulder	chest
back	arm
elbow	waist
hip	leg
knee	foot/feet

Where have you been yesterday?

Alice: Hi, Emma. Where have you been last Sunday?

Emma: I went to Busan. There was a film festival.

Alice: Wow! Were there many actors and actresses?

Emma: Yes. I had chance to see them. All the actresses had big eyes and small faces. Specially, foreign actresses had thin waists and long legs.

Alice: How about the actors?

Emma: All of them looked fantastic. Most of them had wide shoulders and straight noses.

Alice: I feel like going there next year. I hope to see them.

She is _____.

She has _____.

Her _____ is _____ than me.

I can watch TV through _____.

I can hear the song through _____.

I can smell the coffee through _____.

1. When are you free today?

2. What's your father?

3. How do you go to work?

4. Were there many people at the conference?

5. Second quarter profits took a sharp drop!

6. You can do the job by yourself, can't you?

7. Do you go on business trips often?

8. Could you tell her to call me?

9. May I see your license and registration, Sir?

10. Can you finish the report by Friday?

Choosing the correct answer

1. When are you free today?

   (A) I am not free.

   (B) After two o'clock.

   (C) Freedom is valuable.

2. What's your father?

   (A) He is an accountant.

   (B) He likes fishing.

   (C) He can do that.

3. How do you go to work?

   (A) In my car.

   (B) By the subway station.

   (C) At the Wilson bank.

4. Were there many people at the conference?

   (A) Yes, you are.

   (B) Yes, there were.

   (C) Yes, I am full.

5. Second quarter profits took a sharp drop!

   (A) Don't worry. He'll buy you another one.

   (B) This will affect many workers.

   (C) I'm sorry, I took the candies.

6. **You can do the job by yourself, can't you?**

   (A) This is for me, not for you.

   (B) Of course I can. It's a piece of cake.

   (C) No. I'll go there with my friends.

7. **Do you go on business trips often?**

   (A) Yes, I do.

   (B) I'm a business man

   (C) I often go to Seoul.

8. **Could you tell her to call me?**

   (A) Sure, I'll give her the message.

   (B) You can call if you want.

   (C) I am sorry. I don't know

9. **May I see your license and registration, Sir?**

   (A) The authority reduced the license fee.

   (B) Sure. Here you go.

   (C) Why do you think I'm lying to you?

10. **Can you finish the report by Friday?**

   (A) Yes, you can.

   (B) I'll do my best.

   (C) I am very proud of you.

동사(Verb)

의미: 동사는 문장을 완성해 주며, '~다'로 해석한다.

역할: 주어의 행위, 동작, 상태를 나타내며, 문장을 지배하고, 시제를 나타낸다.

1. 동사의 종류: be동사, 조동사, 일반동사

1) be동사: am, are, is로서 기본적인 뜻은 '~이다'와 '있다'로 해석되지만, 문장에서 다양한 역할을 하므로, 특별 동사로 구분된다.

He is a student.

To be or not to be, that is a question.

There is a book on the desk.

2) 조동사: 문장에서 홀로 쓰이지 못하고, 다른 동사와 함께 쓰여 내용을 보충해 주는 역할을 한다. 대표적으로 can/could, will/would, shall/should, may/might, must, need 등이 있다.

I can speak english well.

I will do my best.

We should do study hard.

3) 일반동사: 위 두 경우를 제외하고, '~다'로 문장에서 해석되는 동사로서, 대부분의 동사가 여기에 포함된다.

The man runs very fast.
Anton loves Jane very much.
They gave him a lot of money.

2. 동사의 형태

1) 현재형
주어가 3인칭 단수일 때만 원칙적으로 '-s'나 '-es'를 단어 끝에 붙인다.

I work for the company.
You work for the company.
They work for the company.
He works for the company.

* 동사가 -ch, -sh, -x, -z, -s, -o로 끝나면 '-es'를 붙인다.
watch → watches,   wash → washes,   pass → passes

* 동사가 자음 + y로 끝나면, 'y'를 'i'로 고치고 '-es'를 붙인다.
carry → carries,   study → studies,   marry → marries

2) 과거형 및 과거분사

(1) 규칙변화: 원형에 '-ed'를 붙인다.
wanted, worked, closed, noticed, visited

They worked at the plant yesterday.

Many people wanted to take a trip.

My parents visited me last Sunday.

* 1음절 어에서 모음이 하나일 경우 마지막 자음 하나를 겹쳐 쓴다.

nod - nodded - nodded   stop - stopped - stopped

beg - begged - begged   rob - robbed - begged

* 2음절에서는 둘째 음절에 accent가 있을 때만 자음을 겹친다.

omit - omitted - omitted   admit - admitted - admitted

prefer - preferred - preferred   occur - occurred - occurred

* 「자음 + y」인 경우는 'y' 를 'i'로 고쳐서 '-ed'를 붙인다.

cry - cried - cried   try - tried - tried

study - studied - studied carry - carried - carried

(2) 불규칙변화: 영어에는 약 350여 개 정도의 동사가 불규칙으로 변하고 있으며, 4가지 형태로 나타난다.

ABC형   see - saw - seen   break - broke - broken

ABB형   say - said - said   bring - brought - brought

ABA형   come - came - come   run - ran - run

AAA형   put - put - put   hit - hit - hit

3. 동사의 시제: 12시제

단순	과거 worked	현재 work	미래 will work
완료 have + 과거분사	had worked	have worked	will have worked
진행 be + __ing	was working	am working	will working
완료진행 have been __ing	had been working	have been working	will have been working

1) 현재시제

(1) 현재의 동작

Here comes the teacher.

I go to school.

(2) 현재의 상태

It is very warm today.

He lives in Korea.

(3) 현재의 습관적 동작, 습관, 직업, 성질, 능력

He is often late for school. (습관적 동작)

I get up at six every morning. (습관)

He teaches English. (직업)

She laughs too much. (성질)

She types seventy words a minute. (능력)

(4) 불변의 진리, 사실, 속담

Man is mortal. (사람은 죽게 마련이다)

The sun rises in the east.

(5) 미래의 대용: 왕래발착, 시작 등을 나타내는 동사(go, come, leave, start, begin, start, arrive, return)는 미래를 나타내는 부사(구)와 함께 현재시제로 미래시제를 대신한다.

I start for Busan tomorrow.(= will start)

He comes back next week.(= will come)

The school begins next week.(= will begin)

2) 과거시제

(1) 과거의 동작, 상태

I was born in 1976.

He met his girl friend.

(2) 과거의 습관

He would often go fishing with her.

I met him very often at the bus stop.

(3) 역사적 사실

My teacher asked me when Columbus discovered America.

3) 미래시제

자연현상, 가능(능력), 기대, 감정, 인간의 의지가 포함되지 않은 미래 등.

It will rain tomorrow.

You will be sad.

There will be no school tomorrow.

4) 현재진행

(1) 지금 진행되고 있는 동작

I am reading a novel.

It is raining now.

She's in her room studying.

(2) 미래표시 부사(구)가 왕래발착 동사의 현재 진행형과 함께 쓰이면 가까운 미래를 나타낸다.

He is leaving for America soon.

Where are you spending your next summer vacation?

* be going to + 동사원형의 용법

(1) 가까운 미래: 막 ~하려 하다.(= be about to)

I am going to write a letter.

It's going to rain.

(2) 예정/의도: ~할 작정/예정이다(사전 계획을 통해 미래에 하고자 하는 경우)

I am going to stay here for a week.

I am going to be a doctor.

(3) 미래: ~할 것이다.(= will)

It's going to storm tomorrow.

You are going to see him very often.

5) 과거진행: 과거의 어느 시점에서 진행 중인 동작을 나타낸다.

He was reading a novel when I entered the room.

6) 미래진행: 미래의 어느 시점에서 진행 중인 동작을 나타낸다.

Don't phone me between 7 and 8. We'll be having dinner then.

7) 현재완료: 현재를 기준 시점으로 하여 과거의 어느 시점에서 현재까지의 완료, 결과, 경험, 계속을 나타낸다.

(1) **완료:** 현재에 있어 동작의 완료를 나타낸다. today, this year, recently, just, now, already, by this time, yet, so far 등과 같이 쓰인다.

I have not finished yet.

He has just come back home.

(2) **결과:** 과거 동작에 대한 현재의 결과를 나타낸다.

He has lost his watch.(= He lost his watch and doesn't have it now)

She has bought a new car.(= She bought a new car and has it now)

She has gone to the station.(= She went to the station and is there now)

(3) **경험:** 과거에서 현재까지의 동작, 상태의 경험을 나타낸다. ever, never, before, once, twice, several times, often, seldom 등과 같이 쓰인다.

I have never been to Europe.

Have you ever seen a tiger?

I have met him before.

(4) **계속:** 과거에서 현재까지의 상태의 계속을 나타낸다.

She has been ill since last week.

Five years have passed since he died.

I have known him since he was a child.

8) 과거완료: 과거의 어느 때를 기준점으로 하여 그 이전에 일어난 일의 동작, 혹은 상태의 완료, 결과, 경험, 계속을 나타낸다.

(1) 완료

He had gone to bed when I came to home.
They had arrived at the house before night fell.

(2) 결과

Spring had come by the time she was well again.

(3) 계속

He had lived there for ten years when his mother died.

(4) 경험

I did not know him, for I had never seen him before.

9) 미래완료: 미래의 한 시점을 기준으로 그 때까지 일어난 동작, 혹은 상태의 완료, 결과, 계속, 경험을 나타낸다.

I shall have finished the work by the time you come. (완료)
When you awake, these fancies will have gone. (결과)
I shall have read this book three times if I read it once again. (경험)
I will have been hospital for two weeks by next Sunday. (상태계속)

10) 현재완료 진행: 과거의 어느 시점에서 시작되어 현재 시점에서도 계속되는 동작

He has been studying for ten years.
I have been reading in my study.

11) 과거완료 진행: 과거 이전의 어느 시점에 시작되어 일정 과거 시점에서도 계속되는 동작

I had been waiting for an hour when he returned.

12) 미래완료 진행: 미래의 한 시점에 진행되고 있을 동작

I shall have been reading this novel by noon.

Exercise

A. 밑줄 친 동사의 종류를 구분하세요. (be동사, 조동사, 일반동사)

1. He <u>lives</u> in Seoul.
2. I <u>believe</u> you made a mistake.
3. The man <u>became</u> a famous artist.
4. The foreigner <u>can</u> speak Korean.
5. She has <u>finished</u> her project.
6. Edward <u>was</u> a computer programmer.

B. 밑줄 친 동사의 과거형을 쓰세요.

1. I <u>have</u> a lot of books.
2. She <u>writes</u> Harry Potter.
3. They <u>think</u> he is a doctor.
4. Many people <u>want</u> to see the game.
5. The player <u>hit</u> the ball.
6. I <u>read</u> a history novel.

C. 밑줄 친 동사의 시제를 구분하세요.

1. <u>Have</u> you ever <u>been</u> to America?
2. John <u>is staying</u> in Seoul.
3. She could not sleep well, because she <u>had had</u> much tea.
4. My brother <u>will be</u> there about 2:30.
5. The teacher <u>have been waiting</u> for his son.

조동사(Modal Auxiliary)

> 의미: 조동사는 단어 특성에 따라 의미가 다양하다.
>
> 역할: 문장에서, 주가 되는 일반동사의 의미를 확대시키는 역할을 한다.
>
> 종류: can/could, will/would, shall/should, may/might. must/have
> to, ought, need

1. Can/Could

1) 능력: ~할 수 있다

I can play the piano. (현재) = I am able to play the piano.

I could play the piano. (과거) = I was able to play the piano.

I shall be able to speak English. (미래)

I have been able to speak English. (현재완료)

2) 허가: ~해도 좋다

You can play here.(can = may)

Can I smoke here?

Can I go swimming?

You cannot play here. (금지) (= must not, may not)

You cannot play baseball in the garden. (금지)

3) 요청이나 제안의 표현

Can you give me a ride home?(집에 좀 태워 주시겠습니까?)
* Could you show me the way to the station?(Can보다 공손한 표현)

2. May/Might

1) 허가: ~해도 좋다, ~할 수 있다(= be allowed to ~, be permitted to ~)

You may go there. ↔ You may not go there.
May I use your phone?

2) 현실적 가능성(능력): ~할 수도 있다(= can)

He may know it. ↔ He may not know it. (그는 아마 모를 것이다)
Anyone may see the difference between the two.

3) 추측: ~일지 모른다.

He may be ill. (현재)
He may have been ill. (과거)

4) 기원문

May you be happy!
May he rest in peace!

3. Must/Have to

1) 필요/의무: ~해야 한다

You must do as you are told.(= have to)
You must put on these clothes.(= have to)

2) 강한 추측: ~임에 틀림없다, 반드시 ~일 것이다

He must be ill. ↔ He cannot be ill. (현재)
He must have been ill. ↔ He cannot have been ill. (과거)

3) 필연/불가피: 반드시 ~하다

We must all die sometime.
Sooner or later, death must come to us all!

4. Will/Shall

1) 화자(speaker)의 의지

He shall die.(= I will kill him)
You shall have it.(= I will give it to you)
My son shall bring the money to you.
  (= I will let my son bring the money to you)

2) 청자(hearer)의 의지

Shall my daughter go first?

  (= Do you want me to let my daughter go first?)

Shall he come again?

  (= Will you let him come again?)

Will you lend me the book?

3) 주어의 의지: 인칭에 관계없이 모두 will을 써서, 의지/고집/주장을 나타낸다.

I will do as I like.

Do what you will.

I shall be very glad if you will help me.

She said, "I will leave here."

5. Would

1) 단순/의지 미래의 과거형

He said that he would pay back.

2) will보다 공손한 표현이나 초대, 권유를 나타낸다.

Would you mind opening the door? (공손한 표현)

Would you like some coffee? (권유)

3) 과거의 습관적 행동

He would sit for hours without saying a word. (습관적 행동)
He would often come back drunk, and beat his wife. (습관적 행동)

6. Should

1) 의무/당연: 이 때 'should'는 'must'보다 '의무/당연'의 의미가 약해서 '권고' 또는 '타당함'의 의미를 가지며, had better와 같은 뜻으로 쓰이지만, 그 강도가 'had better'보다 약하다.

Children should obey their parents.(should = ought to)
The young should respect the old.(should = ought to)

2) 가능성/추측(should = ought to)

It should be fine tomorrow.
He should arrive by the 8:00 train.
They should be there by now, I think.

* 주장/명령/요구/제안/충고/권고/결정의 동사 뒤에 이어지는 절에서 should가 쓰인다. 이때 should는 해석되지 않으며, 생략되어 쓰이는 것이 일반적이다.

insist/order, command/desire, require, request, demand, ask/propose, suggest/advise/recommend/decide, determine

I insist that he (should) be sent there.

I propose that the matter (should) be put to the vote at once.

7. Ought to

의무/당연(ought to = should)

He ought to obey his parents.
You ought to start at once.
I told him that he ought to look for her.(= must)

8. Need

1) 긍정문에서 항상 본동사로 쓰이며, 명사나 to부정사를 목적어로 가진다.

He needs to go there.
He needs some money.
He needed to go there.

2) 부정문과 의문문에서 조동사나 본동사로 쓰인다.

He doesn't need to go there. (본동사)
Does he need to go there? (본동사)
He need not go there. (조동사)
He didn't need to go there. (본동사의 과거시제)

§ 다음의 동사들은 문장에서 본래의 뜻은 나타내지 못하고, 문장에서 기능으로만 역할을 할 때가 있으며, 마치 조동사의 역할을 하는 것 같다.

'Do'

1) 강조의 조동사: 본동사 앞에 놓여 본동사를 강조한다.

I do think you ought to go there.
I do wish children weren't so noisy.

2) 의문문과 부정문에서

Do you know him?
You did not finish it.

'Have'

완료구문을 만들기 위해 쓰인다.
I have finished the work already.
A new highway has been built.

'Be'

진행형이나 수동태 구문에서 조동사로 쓰인다.
The president is delivering a speech.
Two large pizzas were delivered.

A. 아래 문장에서 알맞은 것을 고르세요.

1. Eliot (could, must) be on vacation this week.

2. He (might, have to) meet me at the theater.

3. The boy (can, could) attend the English class in the evening.

4. You (could, should) do obey your parents.

5. They insist that he (should, will) be sent there.

6. (May, Must) I borrow your pen?

7. (Can, Will) I ask you a question?

8. (May, Shall) we dance?

9. (Would, Should) you help me?

10. (Could, May) you be quite, please.

Sports

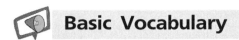

jogging	running
walking	roller skating
cycling	skateboarding
bowling	skydiving
golf	tennis
squash	racquetball
ping pong	handball
baseball	softball
football/soccer	hockey
basketball	volleyball

What do you do in your free time?

Bill: What do you do in your free time?

Andrew: I usually watch TV
  Specially, I like to watch a golf game.

Bill: Do you have any plans for this weekend?
  It will be beautiful day.

Andrew: I don't have any plans for this weekend.

Bill: Good. Let's go to see a baseball game at Chamsil
  Stadium? It will be a big game.

Andrew: That's good. The game will be exciting.
  I need a change.

Individual sports? / Team sports

Indoor sports? / Outdoor sports

A: Which sports do you like to play?

B: I like to play _____.

A: What are the popular sports in your country?

B: I think they are _____.

1. Where can I get the pamphlet?

2. Who's in the movie?

3. Why don't you give me a call tonight?

4. Are you going to open your account?

5. I think I sprained my ankle.

6. Is that for here, or to go?

7. Do you know what today's meeting is on?

8. Can I make a reservation?

9. May I ask as to what you're making?

10. How long does it take from to get your home to the bus stop?

Choosing the correct answer

1. Where can I get the pamphlet?

   (A) You can eat the food.

   (B) At our headquarters.

   (C) It is getting cold.

2. Who's in the movie?

   (A) Bill Foster and Jane Blair.

   (B) It's Steven Spilelberg's.

   (C) I love that movie.

3. Why don't you give me a call tonight?

   (A) I already called you.

   (B) I'll try.

   (C) It is very nice.

4. Are you going to open your account?

   (A) Yes, I am.

   (B) You have a checking account.

   (C) I am an accountant.

5. I think I sprained my ankle.

   (A) That must be painful.

   (B) I often see the anchor on TV.

   (C) Don't worry. The report will be ready by tonight.

6. Is that for here, or to go?

    (A) I'll take it to go.

    (B) I've been here before.

    (C) We have 10 minutes to go into the mall.

7. Do you know what today's meeting is on?

    (A) It's about the effects of office supplies.

    (B) Yes, it's a great piece of work.

    (C) The meeting will be held in room 603.

8. Can I make a reservation?

    (A) Why don't you reserve a seat?

    (B) May I help you?

    (C) What time would you like?

9. May I ask as to what you're making?

    (A) It's a straw hat. Try it on!

    (B) You have to ask by e-mail.

    (C) I don't have time to make it.

10. How long does it take from to get your home to the bus stop?

    (A) I usually take a bus.

    (B) He lives in Long Island.

    (C) About ten minutes.

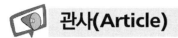 **관사(Article)**

의미: 형용사에 포함되어 있으며, 그 뜻은 기본적으로 '하나의'(a/an) 혹은 '그'(the)로 나타낸다.

역할: 항상 명사 앞에 쓰이며, 그 명사를 한정한다. 종류는 부정관사 'a/an'과 정관사 'the'가 있다.

1. 부정관사 'a/an'

1) one의 약한 뜻으로 보통 해석하지 않는다.

She is an honest girl.

He is a smart boy.

2) '하나'(one의 강한 뜻)

He will finish it in a day or two.

Rome was not built in a day.

Please give me an apple.

3) the same

They are of an age.

Birds of a feather flock together.

of a size(크기가 같은)/of a mind(마음이 맞는)/of a humor(기질이 같은)

4) per(~에, ~마다)

We take three meals a day.
I write to her once a month.
This cloth is 1000 won a yard.

5) any(어떤 ~라도, 모든): 대표단수

A dog is a faithful animal.
A horse is a useful animal.

6) a certain(어떤)의 뜻

A Mr. Jones came to see you.

7) some(어느 정도, 약간)의 뜻

He was speechless for a time. (얼마 동안, 당분간)
Oil paintings look better at a distance. (거리를 두고)

2. 정관사 'the'

1) 앞에 나온 명사를 반복할 경우

The other day I met a boy. The boy was flying a kite.

He lost a purse, and the purse was found in the garbage.

2) 전후관계로 명백히 알 수 있는 경우

Open the door, please.
The post office is near the school.

3) 수식어귀(형용사구, 형용사절)에 의해서 뒤에서 한정될 때: 특정한 것

The principal of our school is Mr. Han.
The water of this well is not good to drink.
She is the girl whom I met yesterday.

4) 유일한 것

The moon is the satellite of the earth.
He traveled around the world.

5) 종족 전체를 나타낼 때(대표단수)

The dog is a faithful animal.
The horse is a useful animal.

6) 서수, 최상급, only, same 앞에서 쓰인다.

I took the first train.
He is the tallest boy in our class.
You are the only student who can do it.

I have the same sharp-pencil as you have.

7) 시간, 수량의 단위를 나타낼 때: by + the + 명사(~로, ~당)

He is paid by the day(week, month).
She rented the apartment by the month.
Sugar is sold by the pound.
Cloth is sold by the yard.

8) 신체의 일부분을 표시할 때

catch, take, hold + 사람(목적격) + by the 신체일부

He caught me by the neck.[by the arm/by the hand]

9) 강, 바다, 해협 등의 이름 앞에

the Thames, the Han River/the Pacific, the Atlantic, the East Sea
/the English Channel, the Straits of Korea, the Magellan Strait.

10) 산맥, 군도, 반도의 이름 앞에

the Alps, the Rocky Mountains/the Philippines, the West Indies
/the Korean Peninsula

3. 관사의 생략

1) 일반적 의미의 불가산명사 및 복수명사 앞에는 관사를 쓰지 않는다.

Water must be pure if it is to be drunk.
Museums are closed on Monday.

2) 호격일 경우

Waiter, give me a cup of coffee.
Father, may I go out?

3) 가족관계일 경우

Mother goes to market in the afternoon.
Father is out, but mother is in.

4) 관직, 신분을 나타내는 말이 동격 또는 보어로 쓰일 때

Elizabeth I, Queen of England, was a great monarch.
They elected him mayor of the city.
He was appointed principal.

5) 명사(건물)가 본래의 목적으로 사용될 때

She goes to church every Sunday.
She goes to the church to see her.

He goes to school every day.

He goes to the school to play baseball.

The man went to prison. (투옥되다)

His wife went to the prison to see him.

6) 식사, 운동, 학과, 질병 이름 앞에

We eat breakfast at seven.

He came immediately after dinner.

He plays tennis every Sunday.

He specializes in mathematics.

He died of cancer.

7) 교통수단

by plane[air](= on a plane)/by train(= on a train)/by ship(= on a ship)/by car(= in a car)/by bus(= on a bus)/by sea(해로로)/on horseback, by coach(마차로)/on foot

8) 통신수단

by telephone/by wireless(무선으로)/by radio(무전으로)/by telegram(전보로)

Exercise

A. 밑줄 친 단어 앞에 관사가 필요하면 써 넣으세요.

1. A dog is <u>faithful</u> animal.
2. I need to <u>teacher</u> to help me.
3. I think she is <u>music</u> dancer.
4. <u>Water</u> is very important.
5. One of my friends lives in <u>Seoul</u>.
6. We should know <u>life</u> is not so long.

B. 밑줄 친 부정관사의 의미를 보기에서 찾아 쓰세요.

보기) one, per, a certain

1. They talked about <u>a</u> movie. _____
2. There is <u>an</u> apple on the table. _____
3. My son usually drink two glasses of milk <u>a</u> day. _____

C. 빈 칸에 알맞은 관사를 써 넣으세요.

1. (   ) caw is a useful animal
2. I don't have (   ) driver's license.
3. Yesterday, I bought an USB, but I lost (   ) USB.
4. Please, open (   ) door.
5. (   ) sun rises in the east.
6. He caught me by (   ) hand.

Fruits & Vegetables

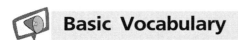

apple	banana	coconut
kiwi	peach	pear
plum	mango	orange
lemon	pineapple	grapes
strawberries	watermelon	
cabbage	celery	lettuce
corn	broccoli	asparagus
spinach	carrot	tomato
potato	sweet potato	radish
onion	green onion	cucumber
mushroom		

When is the Farmer's Market open?

Linda: When is the Farmer's Market open?

Andrew: It is open every Saturday near downtown.

Linda: How about going there this Saturday?
We need apples, cantaloupes, celeries, potatoes and mushrooms. Do they sell fresh fruits and vegetables?

Andrew: Yes, I heard about that. But, the price of them are not so cheap.

Linda: I think there are also some special events at the market.

Andrew: What kinds of events?

Linda: A group concert and a magic show.

Andrew: There will be many people at the market.

My favorite fruit is _____ .

The _____ is a basis vegetables for breakfast.

A: This _____ is delicious?

   Where did you buy it?

B: I bought the _____ at E-mart.

A: Which vegetables do you like?

B: I really like _____ .

1. Where did you go last night?

2. What do you think of my school?

3. How have you been?

4. Are you going to work overtime tonight?

5. You wanted to see me, Mr. Gates?

6. Are you interested in buying or leasing a car?

7. Did you attend the convention?

8. Could you change fifty dollars?

9. May I have a second of your time?

10. How much do I owe you?

Choosing the correct answer

1. Where did you go last night?

(A) I enjoyed it last night.

(B) I went to the new shopping center.

(C) There was an accident last night.

2. What do you think of my school?

(A) I don't think so.

(B) There are many students at the school.

(C) It is very beautiful.

3. How have you been?

(A) Pretty good, thanks.

(B) Thank you, and you?

(C) That sounds good.

4. Are you going to work overtime tonight?

(A) Yes, I have extra hours.

(B) Yes, I have a lot to do.

(C) Yes, I have enough money for it.

5. You wanted to see me, Mr. Gates?

(A) Yes, please step into my office.

(B) Mr. Gates just stepped out.

(C) I don't want to see him any more.

6. Are you interested in buying or leasing a car?

    (A) Yes, I like tuning cars.

    (B) I'd like to lease one.

    (C) I'm sorry. I don't have a car.

7. Did you attend the convention?

    (A) Yes. I'm forced to attend all sales conventions.

    (B) Yes, I can attend the convention.

    (C) Yes, I know where the convention center is.

8. Could you change fifty dollars?

    (A) You have to pay the bill.

    (B) I am going to check out.

    (C) I am afraid not.

9. May I have a second of your time?

    (A) Sure. What's it about?

    (B) Yes. How about this watch?

    (C) Sure thing. It's 10 past 8.

10. How much do I owe you?

    (A) You can pay if you want.

    (B) Forty-five dollars.

    (C) I have only two dollars.

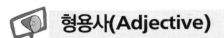

형용사(Adjective)

> 의미: 성질이나 상태를 나타냄.
>
> 역할: 문장에서 명사를 바로 꾸며주거나, 명사를 보충 설명해 주는 역할을 한다.

1. 형용사의 용법

1) 한정용법: 형용사가 명사의 앞 또는 뒤에서 직접 수식하는 것을 말한다.

She is a smart student.

I found an empty box.

2) 서술용법: 형용사가 주어나 목적어를 풀이해 주는 역할을 한다.
즉, 주격보어나 목적격보어로 쓰인다.

The baby is very pretty.

I found him honest.

2. 형용사의 위치

1) 형용사의 어순: 여러 개의 형용사가 올 경우는 대개 다음의 순서를 따른다.
한정사 + 수량(서수/기수) + 대소 + 성상 + 색 + 신구/노소 + 재료/소속/기원

Look at the two large fine old stone houses.

She is a tall thin French lady.

* 한정사: 소유격, 관사, 대명형용사, 부정형용사(some, any, no, little, few, etc.)

2) '-thing', '-body'를 수식하는 형용사는 뒤에서 수식한다.

Please give me something cold to drink.

He is a somebody important.

3. 형용사의 명사 표현

1) the + 형용사: 복수보통명사

The rich stayed the famous hotel.

예) the rich = rich people   the poor = poor people

    the young = young people   the wise = wise people

2) the + 형용사: 추상명사

The woman has an eye the beautiful.

예) the true = truth/the good = good(善)

  /the beautiful = beauty(美)

4. 수사

1) 기수: one, hundred, thousand, million, billion

* dozen, score, hundred, thousand, million 은 복수수사 다음에 쓰여도 's' 를 쓰지 않는다.
  예) three score, two hundred, five million

* 막연히 많은 숫자를 나타낼 때는 복수형을 쓴다.
  예) dozens of people, scores of students, hundreds of people, thousands of people, millions of people

2) 서수: first, second, third, fifth, eighth, ninth, tenth.

3) 분수: 분자는 기수로 분모는 서수로 읽으며, 분자를 먼저 읽고 분모를 읽으며, 분자가 복수일 때는 분모의 서수를 복수형(-s)으로 해주어야 한다.

예) ½: a half or one half, ⅓: one third or a third, ⅔: two thirds
    ¼: one fourth or a quarter,
    134/200: one hundred (and) thirty four over two hundred

4) 소수: 소수점은 point로 읽고, 소수점 뒤의 숫자는 하나씩 따로 읽는다.

1.23: one point two three
0.23: zero point two three
13.704: thirteen point seven zero four

5) 배 수사: once, twice, three times, ten times

This is as large as that.
He has twice the number of my books.
This is three times as large as that.
This is three times the size of that.

6) 연도 등

1991: nineteen ninety-one
1990's: nineteen nineties
387-6077: three eight seven six o double seven

5. 수량형용사

1) Many(수): 많은, + 셀 수 있는 명사

Many students have repeated the same mistakes.

* as many: 동수의
He made ten mistakes in as many lines.
There were five accidents in as many days.

2) Much(양): 많은, + 셀 수 없는 명사

I have much money.

* as much: 동량의

I thought as much.(그 만큼은, 그 정도는)

He drank two bottles of beer and as much wine.

3) Few(수): 조금, + 셀 수 있는 명사
      few(거의 없는: 부정), a few(조금 있는: 긍정)

He has few friends.

He has a few friends.

4) Little(양): 조금, + 셀 수 없는 명사
      little(거의 없는: 부정), a little(조금 있는: 긍정)

I have little money with me.

I have a little money with me.

A. 밑줄 친 형용사가 꾸며주는 명사를 고르세요.

1. I was late at the meeting because of <u>heavy</u> traffic.
2. Something <u>spicy</u> was put into her soup.
3. There is a ugly <u>broken</u> car on the street.
4. I met somebody <u>famous</u> at the mall.
5. My <u>favorite</u> sport is baseball.

B. 밑줄 친 형용사가 설명해 주고 있는 단어(명사 또는 대명사) 또는 구를 고르세요.

1. The city is <u>fantastic</u>.
2. My mother always made me <u>happy</u>.
3. I know he is very <u>smart</u>.
4. I think they believed him <u>honest</u>.

C. 문장에 알맞은 것을 고르세요.

1. I have (a few, a little) breakfast in the morning.
2. He spent (many, much) days doing his project.
3. There is (many, much) snow in this winter.
4. How (many, much) pictures did you take in USA.
5. I don't have (a few, a little) knowledge about it.
6. The man want to get (a few, a little) notebooks.

Everyday Activities

get up	get dressed
brush my teeth	shave
take a shower	make the bed
make breakfast	have breakfast
clean the house	vacuum
wash the dishes	drive a car
do the laundry	watch TV
exercise	make a phone call
return home	go to bed

What do you do in the morning?

Charles: What do you do in the morning?

Andrew: I usually make breakfast and wash the dishes.

Charles: How about in the afternoon?

Andrew: I don't have any plans.

Charles: Me, too. Shall we take a walk at the civic park. It is beautiful outside.

Andrew: Good! I need to exercise.

Charles: See you at 12 at the park.

Andrew: O.K. See you there.

I _____ before having breakfast.

I _____ after having lunch.

A: What do you do in the morning?

B: I _____ in the morning.

A: What are you doing?

B: I am _____.

1. When is our next holiday?

2. Whose is the beef steak?

3. How long have you been here?

4. Is he good at algebra?

5. Keep your eyes on my bag, please.

6. Which is best for you, blue or white?

7. Did you happen to see the news on TV?

8. Could you tell me where the post office is?

9. May I introduce my friend Mr. Porter to you?

10. Would you like any dessert?

Choosing the correct answer

1. When is our next holiday?

   (A) I'd like to go to Europe this holiday.

   (B) In three weeks, on Wednesday, the 20th.

   (C) You should go to the States during Christmas.

2. Whose is the beef steak?

   (A) I ordered.

   (B) She is in the kitchen.

   (C) Well done, please.

3. How long have you been here?

   (A) For half an hour.

   (B) I have been there twice.

   (C) I have a long story.

4. Is he good at algebra?

   (A) No, he has no allergies.

   (B) No, he got a C in math.

   (C) Yes, he likes zebras.

5. Keep your eyes on my bag, please.

   (A) I'm sorry, I put the bag in your car.

   (B) Where're you going?

   (C) The bag is kept in Lost and Found.

6. Which is best for you, blue or white?

(A) I like them very much.

(B) I think the blue one is bigger.

(C) I'll buy the one you recommend.

7. Did you happen to see the news on TV?

(A) No, why? Is it something important for us?

(B) Yes, the newspaper is delivered in the evening.

(C) Yes, I have a new high-definition flat-screen TV.

8. Could you tell me where the post office is?

(A) You can mail it.

(B) I'm sorry. I don't have it.

(C) Turn right at the next corner.

9. May I introduce my friend Mr. Porter to you?

(A) You don't need to. I already know him.

(B) Yes. The introduction of the article is impressive.

(C) No, not at all.

10. Would you like any dessert?

(A) I am sorry. I don't have.

(B) No, thank you. I am full.

(C) Sure, It's time to go.

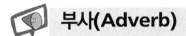 부사(Adverb)

의미: 성질, 상태, 동작, 문장 등의 의미를 보다 분명하게 함.
역할: 문장에서 동사, 형용사, 부사 또는 문장 전체를 수식한다.
시간, 장소, 방법, 정도, 빈도 등을 나타낸다.

1. 부사의 기능

1) 동사 수식

He speaks English well.
He did not die happily.

2) 형용사 수식

She is very clever.
This is too expensive.

3) 부사 수식

They lived very happily.

4) 문장 전체 수식

Happily he did not die.

Unfortunately he died.

Probably he will succeed this time.

2. 부사 형태

1) 형용사에다가 '-ly'를 붙인다.

slow - slowly   careful - carefully   glad - gladly

2) 형용사와 같은 형태의 부사: early, long, hard, enough, fast, pretty, late, high 등은 형용사와 부사의 형태가 같다.

The early bird catches the worm.

I get up early in the morning.

She wrote a long letter to her teacher.

He was long ill.

He has money enough for his trip.

She is old enough to love.

He is fast runner.

He eats fast.

3) 형용사와 같은 형태의 부사와 -ly형의 부사가 뜻이 서로 다른 경우가 있다.

It is hard to understand. (어려운)

He studies hard. (열심히)

He hardly studies. (거의 않는)

I was late for school today.

The doctor came too late.

I haven't seen him lately.

She is pretty. (귀여운)

He is pretty well now. (상당히, 꽤)

She is prettily dressed. (예쁘게)

Mt. Baegdu is very high.

The cat can jump high.

It is a highly interesting movie. (굉장히)

3. 부사의 위치

1) 빈도부사의 위치

　종류: always, never, often, sometimes, seldom, rarely, scarcely, regularly, ever, usually

　위치: 빈도부사 + 일반동사

　　　 be동사 + 빈도부사

　　　 조동사 + 빈도부사 + 본동사

He is always at home.

I have never been to England.

I can scarcely understand his words.

It seldom snows in Busan.

* 여러 개의 낱말로 이루어진 구 형태의 빈도부사는 문미나 문두에 위치한다.
now and then, from time to time, on occasion, all the time, twice a week, now and again, every two days

I go to the language school every two days.

2) 장소 + 방법 + 시간
시간부사어구: 작은 단위 + 큰 단위
장소부사어구: 좁은 장소 + 넓은 장소
일반부사(구): 짧은 부사(구) + 긴 부사(구)

I'll visit you at seven o'clock next Sunday.
We arrived safely at the station.
He arrived there safely yesterday.
We lived there happily before.
I met him at the station at five o'clock.

4. 주의해야 할 부사의 용법

1) enough: 일반적으로 부사가 형용사, 부사를 수식할 때는 형용사 앞에 놓이는 것이 원칙이지만, enough는 수식하는 말 뒤에 놓인다.

He does not work enough.
He is rich enough to buy the Volvo.

2) only: 관계가 가장 밀접한 것과 가까이 두는 것이 원칙이다.

Only I can see him in the room.
I can only see him in the room.
I can see only him in the room.
I can see him only in the room.

3) already와 yet
already는 긍정문에 사용: 이미, 벌써

Linda has already gone to bed.
Has the bell rung already?

yet은 의문문, 부정문에 사용

Has the bell rung yet? (벌써, 이미)
The work is not yet finished. (아직)

* 긍정문에 yet가 사용되면: 아직, 여전히
She is talking yet.

4) ago와 before
ago: 현재를 기준으로 하여 '지금부터 ~전'의 뜻. 항상 과거시제에 사용
before: 과거를 기준으로 하여 '그때부터 ~전'의 뜻. 주로 과거완료에 사용

My father died ten years ago.
I had received a letter three days (ago, before).
When I met him two years ago, he said his son had died five years

before.

5) 유도부사 there: 문두에서 동사를 이끄는 역할을 한다.

There is a book.

There is no one there.

There used be a bridge here.

There seems to have been a fire.

A. 밑줄 친 부사가 꾸며주는 것을 찾으세요.

1. The doctor talks <u>very</u> fast.
2. <u>Unfortunately</u>, he was absent.
3. He is old <u>enough</u> to take a trip by himself.
4. I slept <u>deeply</u> yesterday.
5. My son learns language <u>quickly</u>.

B. 주어진 부사(구)를 문장에 알맞게 써 넣으세요.

1. She gets up early in the morning. (usually)
2. He is rich to buy the car. (enough)
3. Tom can speak English. (well)
4. I used to go shopping with my husband. (all the time)
5. I am happy to meet you. (really)

C. 밑줄 친 단어의 뜻을 쓰세요.

1. The bus arrived ten minutes <u>late</u>.
2. I haven't seen him <u>lately</u>.
3. The man is working <u>hard</u>.
4. He <u>hardly</u> ever go to church.
5. The cat can jump <u>high</u>.
6. It is a <u>highly</u> interesting movie.

Place around town

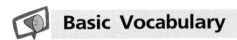

convenience store	bank
bakery	cafeteria
clinic/hospital	hotel
day care center	cleaners/laundry
department store	drug store/pharmacy
concert hall	museum
movie theater	library
gas station	grocery store
laundromat	parking lot
post office	police station
restaurant	train station

Where are you going?

Linda: Hi, how are you today?

Andrew: Pretty good. Where are you going?

Linda: I am going to a department store. There is a big sale at the store. Do you want to join me?

Andrew: I really want to, but I am going to the city library. I have to read a special book.

Linda: Is the library open today? It's Sunday!

Andrew: Yes, it is. The cafeteria next to the library is also open today. I will have lunch at the cafeteria. Enjoy your shopping!

Linda: See you tomorrow.

Is there a/an _____ nearby?

There is a/an _____ around the school.

A: Where are you going?

B: I am going to the _____.

A: Where is the _____?

B: It is next to the _____.

1. Where can I check out?

2. What's the date today?

3. How long does it take to fix the machine?

4. Are you ready to go?

5. Care for a drink at the bar?

6. Would you rather leave today or tomorrow?

7. Do you have time for a cup of coffee?

8. Would you like a round-trip ticket?

9. Have you read the new income tax law?

10. Can you play the piano?

Choosing the correct answer

1. **Where can I check out?**

   (A) You don't need to check.

   (B) At the front desk.

   (C) He is out.

2. **What's the date today?**

   (A) It's very cold today.

   (B) It's the end of the month.

   (C) It's Monday.

3. **How long does it take to fix the machine?**

   (A) Just two hours.

   (B) It's very long.

   (C) The machine is very expensive.

4. **Are you ready to go?**

   (A) Yes, I am.

   (B) Yes, I will buy the radio.

   (C) I am reading.

5. **Care for a drink at the bar?**

   (A) I'm stuffed, I think I'll pass.

   (B) No thanks, I have a stomachache.

   (C) Good! I like the chocolate bar, too.

6. Would you rather leave today or tomorrow?

   (A) I'll stop by at 3 tomorrow.

   (B) I'd rather not live with you.

   (C) Today would be better.

7. Do you have time for a cup of coffee?

   (A) I have been there many times.

   (B) Yes, I want you to buy the cup.

   (C) Yes, I really want to have a good time with you.

8. Would you like a round-trip ticket?

   (A) The table is rounded.

   (B) The ticket is very expensive.

   (C) Yes, please.

9. Have you read the new income tax law?

   (A) Yes, the taxi was so comfortable.

   (B) No, but I know it is very ambiguous.

   (C) My annual income has been increasing since 2008.

10. Can you play the piano?

    (A) Yes, I like snow.

    (B) Yes, I took lessons for two years.

    (C) Of course. I can carry it.

접속사(Conjunction)

의미: 같은 단위를 연결

역할: 단어와 단어, 구와 구, 절과 절을 연결한다.

1. 등위접속사

1) 완전등위접속사: 완전히 대등한 단문이나 구를 연결시키는 접속사를 말한다.

  (1) 'and'
    - 단일 개념을 나타낸다.

Time and tide wait(s) for no man.

Slow and steady wins the race.

Bread and butter is my favorite breakfast.

    - 부정사 대신에 쓰는 경우: go, come, try, send, run, mind, write 등의
                       다음에 오는 and는 to 부정사의 대용으로 쓰여
                       '목적(~하기 위해서)'의 의미를 가진다.

Come and see me.(= Come to see me)

Try and use plain words.(= Try to use plain words)

- 명령문 + and: ~하라, 그러면

Work hard, and you will succeed.
Push the button, and the door will open.

(2) 'but'
Excuse me, but what is your name?

(3) 'or'
  - or: 말하자면, 즉(= that is, that is to say)
I weigh 110 pounds or about 50 kilograms.

  - 명령문 + or = unless, if ~ not(~하라, 그렇지 않으면)
Work hard, or you will fail.(= Unless you work hard, you will fail.)

2) 등위 상관접속사

Either you or I am to blame. (A 또는 B 둘 중의 하나)
He can neither ski nor swim. (A와 B 둘 다 아닌)
Both butter and cheese are nutritious foods. (A와 B 둘 다)

* not only A but (also) B = B as well as A(A뿐만 아니라 B 역시)
Not only you but also I was wrong. = You as well as I are wrong.
Not money but wisdom is what I want. (A가 아니고 B인)

2. 종속접속사

1) 명사절을 이끄는 접속사

(1) 'That': 주로 단정적인 내용을 이끈다.

  - 주절, 목적절, 주격보어절을 이끈다.

That he has gone is certain. (주절)

I think it a pity that you didn't try harder. (목적절)

The trouble is that we are short of money. (주격보어절)

(2) 'whether': '~인지 어떤지(아닌지)'의 의미로 양자택일을 요하는 문장을 이
      끈다.

  - 주절을 유도

It is very doubtful whether he will consent (or not). (진주어절)

Whether he is wise or stupid is not important problem.

  - 목적절을 유도(whether = if)

I wonder whether the news is true.

I don't know whether he is at home or at the office.

I am not sure whether he will pass the final test (or not).

2) 부사절을 이끄는 접속사

  - 시간의 부사절을 이끄는 접속사

(1) 'when/as/whenever'

When her husband had an accident, she was coming home for work.

Give her this letter when she comes. (~할 때에, ~하면(= if))

They were about to start fighting when their father intervened. (바로 그때)

He came up as she was speaking. (~할 때(= when))

Whenever I felt lonely, I used to visit his house. (~할 때는 언제나)

(2) 'until'

~할 때까지

We stayed there until we finished our work.

(3) 'before'

긍정문 + before: ~해서야(지나서야) 비로소 ~하다

It will be long before he notices it.

    (한참 지나서야 그가 알게 될 것이다)

It was five years before I met Jane again.

    (5년이 지나서야 비로소 Jane을 다시 만났다)

(4) 'after'

I'll go after I finish my work.

(5) 'since': ~이후로, ~이래로

Five years have passed since his father died.

He came to New York two years ago and has lived here ever since.

– 이유/원인의 부사절을 이끄는 접속사

(1) 'because': 직접적인 이유/원인을 나타낸다.

He could finish the work because he worked hard.

I did not go because I wanted to.(내가 원해서 간 것은 아니었다)

(2) 'since': because보다 의미가 약하며, 간접적인 이유/원인을 나타낸다.

Since no one agrees to my proposal, I will give it up.

(3) 'for': because보다 의미가 약하며, comma 뒤에 쓰여서 추가[보충]적 이유
/원인을 설명한다.

She was sleeping, for she worked all day.(for=because)

(4) 'as': since보다 의미가 약하며, 간접적인 이유/원인을 나타낸다.

As it was cold yesterday, I stayed home all day.

– 목적의 부사절을 이끄는 접속사

(so) that ~ may[can] = in order that ~ may[can]: ~하기 위하여

He worked hard so that he might succeed.

I packed her some food (so) that he wouldn't get hungry.

– 결과의 부사절을 이끄는 접속사

so + 형용사/부사 + that ~/such + a(an) + 형용사 + 명사 + that ~: 너무 ~해서
~하다

It was so hot that we went swimming.

It was such a nice weather that we went out for a walk.

– 양보의 부사절을 이끄는 접속사

(1) though = although = even though

Though he is poor, he is happy.[although 보다는 구어적인 의미를 가짐]

Even though I don't love her, I have to marry her.(비록 ~라 하더라도)

(2) if/even if

If he is poor, he is a nice guy.

Even if we are not rich, we have good friends.

– 장소의 부사절을 이끄는 접속사(where/wherever)

God knows where he comes from.

Go wherever you want to go.

– 양태의 부사절을 이끄는 접속사

(1) as: ~처럼, ~대로

Do in Rome as the Romans do.

As you treat me, so will I treat you.

(2) as if/as though: 마치 ~처럼

He talks as if he knew everything.

– 조건을 이끄는 접속사(if)

If it's cold tomorrow, I will stay at home.

A. 문장에서 접속사가 연결하고 있는 것에 밑줄 치세요.

1. I want to buy apples and tomatoes at the shop.
2. We should take this bus or wait for next one.
3. Tom lost his wallet, but his wife found it at the park.
4. To be or not to be, that is a question.

B. 빈칸에 알맞은 단어를 써 넣으세요.

1. (　　) she (　　) I were satisfied with the result.
2. (　　) John or Jane will be a first player.

C. 접속사가 이끄는 절에 밑줄을 치세요.

1. He told me that he couldn't take the position.
2. My wife asked if I wanted to have lunch at home.
3. Mike thought that I had made a mistake.
4. I wonder whether Linda told a lie.
5. That she is honest is clear.

의미: 다른 품사 단어, 구 절 앞에 놓여, 그 의미를 나타냄.

1. 전치사의 목적어

전치사 뒤에 나오는 단어, 구, 절 등을 전치사의 목적어라 한다. 전치사의 목적어로는 명사, 대명사, 형용사, 과거분사, 부사, 동명사, 부정사, 구, 절이 올 수 있다.

1) 명사, 대명사

He goes to school by bus.
He lives with Tom.
Let's play with them.
I bought a pencil for him.

* 전치사의 목적어로 대명사가 올 때는 반드시 목적격을 써주어야 한다.

2) 형용사, 과거분사, 부사

Things went from bad to worse.
You should not take your parent's sacrifice for granted.

He returned from abroad.

It is far from here.

3) 동명사, 부정사

He is fond of driving in the country.

He is afraid of going alone.

There is nothing but to wait.

I was about to leave.

4) 구

He appeared from behind the tree.

He read the book till late at night.

5) 절

From where I was sitting I could not see them.

He will not work except when he is pleased.

2. 전치사의 종류

1) 장소를 나타내는 전치사

at: 비교적 좁은 장소에 사용.

in: 넓은 장소에 사용.

I live at Chongro in Seoul.

He is standing at the door.

I was staying at a hotel in New York.

on: 접촉하여 '위에'

above: 막연한 '위로'(보다 높이)

beneath: 접촉하여 '아래에'

below: 막연한 '아래로'(보다 아래로)

over: 수직으로 바로 '위에'

up: 밑에서 '위(쪽으)로'

under: 수직으로 바로 '아래에'

down: 위에서 '아래(쪽으)로'

There is a vase on the table.

The ice gave way beneath our feet.

The moon has risen above the horizon.

The sun has just sunk below the horizon.

A jet plane flew over the city.

He was lying under the tree.

They went up and down the street.

We sailed down the river.

between: 둘 사이에

among: 셋 이상 사이에

There is a river between the two villages.

Many birds are singing among the trees.

behind: ~의 뒤에   Who is the man behind the tree?

after: 뒤를 쫓아   The dog ran after the rabbit.

in: ~의 안에   I study in this room.

into: ~의 안으로   He came into the room.

out of: ~의 밖으로   He came out of the room.

across: ~을 가로질러, ~을 횡단하여

through: ~을 통과하여

along: ~에 연하여, ~을 따라서

    He came across the street.

    The train passed through the tunnel.

    We walked along the river.

round: ~의 주위에(주위를 도는 운동 상태)

around: ~의 주위에(주위에 정지한 상태)

about: ~의 주위에(막연한 주변, 여기저기)

    The earth moves round the sun.

    We sat around the bonfire.

    He walked about the park.

to: ~로(도착지점을 표시)

for: ~방향으로(행선지나 목적지를 표시)

from: ~에서(출발지점을 표시)

toward: ~의 방향으로(막연한 목표를 표시)

    He has gone to England.

    He left Seoul for L.A.

    The train is for Busan.

    He started from Seoul

    He bowed toward England.

2) '때'를 나타내는 전치사

at: 시각이나 시점 등 짧은 시간을 나타낸다(몇 시, 몇 분, 밤, 정오, 새벽).

on: 일정한 날짜, 요일, 정해진 시간의 아침, 오전, 오후를 나타낸다.

in: at보다 긴 시간을 나타낸다(년, 월, 계절, 세기, 아침, 저녁, 오후).

at six, at night, at noon, at dawn(= daybreak), at midnight.

on Sunday, on New Year's Day, on May 10th, on the morning of 11th

in April, in Autumn, in 1945, in the 20th Century

till: '~까지'(어느 때까지의 동작의 계속을 나타낸다)

by: '~까지'(어느 때까지의 동작의 완료를 나타낸다)

before: '전에'(어느 때 이전에 동작의 완료를 나타낸다)

I will stay here till five.

I will come here by five.

I will be at that restaurant till you come.

I will finish my work by five.

I usually finish work before six.

in: '~이 지나면'(시간의 경과를 나타낸다. 미래시제가 중심임)

within: '~이내에'(일정한 기간이내를 나타낸다)

after: '~후에'(과거부터)

She will be back in a few days.

Cancer will kill him in a few weeks.

He will come back within a couple of days.

He came back after few days.

3) 원인/이유의 전치사

for: ~때문에

from: 직접적인 원인(피로, 부상, 과로 등에 의한)

of: 행위의 원인(~으로: 사망, 병)

The boss will blame you for neglecting your job.

He fell ill from drinking too much.

He died from overwork.

4) 원료/재료의 전치사

of: '~으로 만들어 지다'[물리적 변화 - 형태는 변해도 질은 변하지 않는 경우]

from: '~으로 만들어 지다[화학적 변화 - 형태와 질이 모두 변하는 경우]

in: 표현방법, 수단, 재료

The bridge is built of wood.

The house was made of wood.

Wine is made from grapes.

Beer is made from barley.

This picture is painted in oils.

You must write letters in ink.

Speak in English.

Look at the woman in white.

5) 수단/도구의 전치사

by: '~에 의해서'(행위자), '~을 타고'(운송수단)

with: '~을 가지고, ~으로'(도구)

through: '~을 통하여'(중개, 매개수단)

The novel was written by Hemingway

He traveled by train.

He cut bread with knife.

Write it with a pen.

I looked at the moon through a telescope.

We get knowledge through books.

A. 문장에서 전치사와 한 묶음이 되는 것에 밑줄을 치세요.

1. The USB in the box is expensive.
2. She went to the post office.
3. They usually play soccer at the school.
4. I haven't seen my son in one year.

B. 빈 칸에 알맞은 전치사를 써 넣으세요.

1. I don't have a pen to write (   ).
2. Candy is (   ) Austria
3. He will meet me (   ) Sunday.
4. I will be back (   ) five o'clock.
5. There are a lot of books (   ) the desk.
6. The police station is (   ) the corner of the street.
7. The chair is made (   ) wood.

Numbers & Calendar

Basic Vocabulary

first   second   third   fourth   fifth

sixth   seventh   eighth   ninth   tenth

eleven   twelve   thirteen   fourteen   fifteen

sixteen   seventeen   eighteen   nineteen   twenty

thirty   forty   fifty   sixty   seventy

eighty   ninety   hundred   thousand   million

January   February   March   April

May   June   July   August

September   October   November   December

Sunday   Monday   Tuesday   Wednesday

Thursday   Friday   Saturday

January is the first month of the year.

Linda: Do you have new plans for your health?

Andrew: Yes. I made my plan. It is January, the first month of year. How about you?

Linda: I bought a winter swimming ticket. It costs 200$ for three months.

Andrew: How often do you go to the swimming center?

Linda: I go there on Monday, Wednesday and Friday. Three times a week.

Andrew: It will be good for your health. I bought a monthly exercise ticket. I paid 40$ for a month. I usually go to the center after work.

The tree is _____ years old.

I live on the _____ floor.

A: What month is it?

B: It is _____.

A: What day is it?

B: It is _____.

1. When was the last time you saw a movie?

2. By whom was the system developed?

3. Why don't you take a taxi?

4. Is there a directory in this shopping mall?

5. Be careful not to touch this switch.

6. Is this a new battery, or is it trash?

7. Did you bump your head?

8. Will you be back in time for the party?

9. Have you notified our clients of new products?

10. Where did you park your van?

Choosing the correct answer

1. When was the last time you saw a movie?
   (A) I saw them with my friends.
   (B) Last Christmas at the TGV Cinema.
   (C) I'm sorry. I don't have the time.

2. By whom was the system developed?
   (A) By our R&D Institution.
   (B) By the window.
   (C) It was AT&T that bought the system.

3. Why don't you take a taxi?
   (A) That's a good idea.
   (B) It's too late.
   (C) I'm not a taxi driver.

4. Is there a directory in this shopping mall?
   (A) I don't know where the mall is.
   (B) I think you have to call information.
   (C) There's a dictionary in my bag.

5. Be careful not to touch this switch.
   (A) Don't worry. I won't.
   (B) Switch the phone over to me, please.
   (C) Yes, I'll have a sandwich.

6. Is this a new battery, or is it trash?

   (A) That's rechargeable. Put that in the drawer.

   (B) The trash bin in under the desk.

   (C) Actually, this battery is better than that.

7. Did you bump your head?

   (A) Yes. I bumped into him in the city hall.

   (B) Yes. The ceiling is too low.

   (C) No. There weren't any speed bumps.

8. Will you be back in time for the party?

   (A) The party was very good.

   (B) It's time to start.

   (C) I'm not sure. But I'll try.

9. Have you notified our clients of new products?

   (A) No, I'm not his client.

   (B) No, that's Jane's responsibility.

   (C) Yes, the products are very nice.

10. Where did you park your van?

    (A) Across from the drug store.

    (B) The parking lot is over there.

    (C) I am a big fan of the singer.

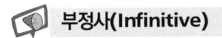 # 부정사(Infinitive)

의미: 동사의 뜻을 그대로 가지고 있으며, 문장에서 다른 품사처럼 쓰인다.

역할: 문장에서 명사, 형용사, 부사처럼 쓰인다.

형태: to + 동사원형

부정사 부정: 부정사 바로 앞에 부정어를 둔다.

1. 명사적 용법

1) 주어의 역할

To live long is the desire of all men.

To know oneself is difficult.

To work hard is the best way to success.

2) 목적어의 역할(타동사의)

He promised to go there.

He promised me to return at there.

She wants to study English.

3) 보어의 역할

To live is to suffer. (주격보어)

To see her is to love her.

Our wish is to preserve peace.

You have to persuade him to help the poor child. (목적격보어)

She allowed me to play with it.

We all expected him to come here.

4) 명사구(의문사 + to 부정사)

I don't know where to go.

I don't know when to do it.

I don't know whom to go with.

I wondered how to contact them.

I don't know whether to go or turn back.

5) 진주어/진목적어로서

To make ourselves understood is not easy.

　　→ It is not easy to make ourselves understood.

To work hard is the best way to success.

　　→ It is the best way to success to work hard.

I make to get up at six every morning a rule.

　　→ I make it a rule to get up at six every morning.

6) 동격

His ambition, to be a pilot, was never fulfilled.
He has one aim, to make money.

2. 형용사적 용법

1) 한정적 용법

I have no friend to help me.
He is not a person to break his promise.
He is the very man to do this work.
I have no family to look after me.
I bought a book to read on the plane.
There is no time to lose now.
I have a letters to write.
He has many children to look after.

2) 서술적 용법(보어역할)

He seems to be honest. (주격보어)
He appears to be honest. (주격보어)
I chanced to meet her in my walk. (주격보어)
I knew him to be diligent.
I told him to do his best.

* 'be + to 원형동사'의 용법: 이때 'to + 원형동사'는 보어가 된다.

(1) 예정(~할 예정이다 = be due to, be scheduled to)

We are to meet him here.

The meeting is to be held tomorrow.
He is to make a speech next Monday.

(2) 의무/명령(~해야 한다.)

You are to start at once.
You are to obey the law.

(3) 가능(~할 수 있다): 주로 부정문이나 수동태에 사용된다.

Nothing was to be seen.
My house is to be seen from the station.

(4) 운명(~할 운명이다 = be destined to, be doomed to, be fated to)

The poet was to die young.
He was never to see his wife again.

(5) 목적/의도(~하고자 하다 = intended to): 주로 조건절에서 쓰인다.

If you are to succeed, you must work hard.
If you are to catch the train, you had better hurry.

3. 부사적 용법

1) 목적: 동작의 목적을 나타낸다. '~하기 위해서'의 뜻으로 해석

We eat to live, not live to eat.

He raised his right hand to ask a question.

He works hard to succeed in life.

2) 결과: 동작의 결과를 나타낸다.

He lived to see his great-grandchildren.

He grew up to be a great poet.

He worked hard only to fail.

He left his home, never to return.

3) 원인: 감정을 나타내는 동사나 형용사 다음에 오는 부정사는 원인을 나타내며, '~하니', '~해서'의 뜻으로 번역된다.

I am very glad to see you.

I feel sorry to hear of his failure.

He was happy to see his wife again.

I was surprised to find him dead.

She wept to see the sight.

4) 이유, 판단의 근거: '~을 보니', '~을 하다니'로 해석

He is a happy man to have such a good son.

He must be a fool to say such a thing.

He cannot be rich to ask you for some money.
What a foolish he is to believe such a thing!
How foolish I was to trust him!

5) 조건: '만일 ~이면'

To hear him speak English, one would take him for an American.
I should be glad to go with you.

6) 양보: '~할지라도', '비록 ~하여도'

To see it, you would not believe it.
To do his best, he could not succeed in it.

4. 원형부정사('to'가 없이 동사원형만 쓰는 경우)

1) 사역동사 다음에 원형부정사가 쓰인다. 이 때 원형부정사는 목적보어가 된다.

종류: have, make, let, (help)
Father made me turn off the radio.
I will have him wash the car.
He made me do it.
He let her attend the party.
I will help you (to) do the work. (영국식에서는 to를 쓰기도 한다)

2) 지각동사 다음에도 원형부정사가 쓰인다. 이 때 원형 부정사는 목적보어가 된다.

종류: see, hear, feel, watch, listen to, smell

I heard her play the piano in the concert.

I saw him enter the house.

I did not notice him go upstairs.

They observed the birds come back to their nests one by one.

They listened to me speak.

I felt myself tremble with the cold.

5. 부정사의 의미상의 주어

1) 주어가 부정사의 의미상의 주어인 경우

I expect to pass the examination.

He longed to get the prize.

I want to read this novel.

2) 목적어가 부정사의 의미상의 주어인 경우

I expect you to pass the examination.

He told me to work hard.

I advise you to stop smoking.

He allowed me to do so.

He proved it to be true.

3) 의미상의 주어가 '일반인'일 때는 명시하지 않는다.

It is not easy (for us) to learn a foreign language.

4) 사람의 성질이나 특징을 나타내는 형용사 다음에 오는 부정사의 의미상의 주어는 'of + 목적어'를 쓴다.

종류: kind, good, generous, nice, foolish, wise, careful, careless, rude, stupid, silly, polite, bad, cruel.

It is rude of you to speak in that way.

It is very kind of you to say so.

Exercise

A. 아래 문장에서 부정사를 확인하고, 그 용법(명사, 형용사, 부사)을 표시하세요.

1. To see is very important in life.

2. I don't have time to read the book.

3. He wants to have lunch with him.

4. I don't know what to do.

5. We have to do our best to win the game.

6. I am glad to see you again.

B. 각 문장에서 밑줄 친 부정사의 의미상의 주어를 확인하세요.

1. Tom wanted to see me yesterday.

2. It is very kind of you to say so.

3. It is very hard for him to get up early in the morning.

4. They told me to meet you here.

5. The man stepped aside for the lady to pass.

C. 문장에 알맞은 것을 고르세요.

1. I saw him (to enter, enter) the classroom.

2. It is impossible (for me, of me) to swim in the river.

3. Jane had him (to finish, finish) the computer game.

4. Let me (look at, to look at) the bag.

5. Do you know what (do, to do) next?

Weather & Seasons

winter	spring
summer	autumn/fall
warm	cool
cold	freezing
sunny	clear
cloudy	windy
foggy	humid
raining	hailing
snowing	
lightning	tornado
snowstorm	thunderstorm
typhoon	
fahrenheit	centigrade

Winter is a ski season!

Linda: What's the weather forecast?

Andrew: It will be sunny tomorrow.

Linda: That's great! Let's go skiing tomorrow.

Andrew: The road condition will be good to drive.

Linda: There are a lot of snow at the mountain.

Andrew: It will be cold at the mountain. We have to take extra winter parkers.

Linda: That's good idea. Mountains are usually much colder than downtown.

Andrew: It will be exciting tomorrow.

Linda: Winter is a ski season. I have wanted to see lots of snow this winter.

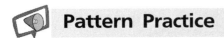

My favorite season is _____ because _____.

It will be _____ tomorrow.

A: How is the weather?

B: It is _____.

A: How is the temperature?

B: It is ten degrees _____.

1. Where can I leave my bag?

2. What are you going to do this weekend?

3. How are things going at work?

4. Are you going out for lunch?

5. Don't forget about the accounting department meeting at 7.

6. Don't you think we should call a repairman?

7. Do you think this business would be profitable?

8. Would you like some more ice cream?

9. Have you ever been to Boston?

10. Can I make a reservation?

Choosing the correct answer

1. **Where can I leave my bag?**

   (A) Put it in the closet.

   (B) I live on third street.

   (C) The bag is big.

2. **What are you going to do this weekend?**

   (A) The weather will be fine this weekend.

   (B) There is a big game this Saturday.

   (C) I am going to be a good player.

3. **How are things going at work?**

   (A) Pretty well.

   (B) Everybody is going to work.

   (C) I am going to see a movie.

4. **Are you going out for lunch?**

   (A) No, I am going to order in.

   (B) I didn't have lunch yet.

   (C) I will have pizza, please.

5. **Don't forget about the accounting department meeting at 7.**

   (A) Really? I was planning to leave early.

   (B) I'm not good at mathematics.

   (C) I never forget his name.

6. Don't you think we should call a repairman?

   (A) Yes, we don't need to call the repairman.

   (B) Yes, we need money.

   (C) Yes, the problem is serious.

7. Do you think this business would be profitable?

   (A) It's very competitive, but it will be.

   (B) Our profit rate grew by only 10 percent.

   (C) Yes, it opens next month.

8. Would you like some more ice cream?

   (A) Thanks. I don't have it.

   (B) Yes, I'll get you some.

   (C) No, thanks. I'm full.

9. Have you ever been to Boston?

   (A) Yes, it is.

   (B) I have been there twice.

   (C) One of my friends is from Boston.

10. Can I make a reservation?

    (A) He reserved it.

    (B) Yes, you can.

    (C) You can't see the cafe.

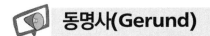 **동명사(Gerund)**

의미: 동사의 뜻을 그대로 가지고 있으며, 문장에서 다른 품사처럼 쓰인다.

역할: 문장에서 동사적 성질을 갖고, 명사 역할을 한다.

형태: 동사원형 + ing

동명사 부정: 동명사 바로 앞에 부정어를 둔다.

1. 동명사의 역할

1) 주어

Travelling by car is very interesting.

Seeing is believing.

2) 목적어

She began crying bitterly.

I don't like swimming in the river.

She is proud of being a beauty. (전치사의 목적어)

I am fond of swimming. (전치사의 목적어)

3) 보어

My hobby is collecting foreign stamps.

My dream is meeting the poet.

It is throwing your money away.

* **동명사와 현재분사의 구별**

  현재분사: 상태나 동작을 나타내어 '~하고 있는'의 뜻

  동명사: 목적이나 용도를 나타내며 '~하기 위하여'의 뜻

  a sleeping baby = a child who is sleeping

  a sleeping car = a car used for sleeping

  a waiting lady = a lady who is waiting

  a waiting room = a room for waiting

2. 동명사의 의미상의 주어

  의미상의 주어가 문장 주어와 같을 때는 생략하고, 문장주어와 다를 때는 그 의미상의 주어를 써 주어야 한다. 그러나 문장주어와는 다르지만 그 문장의 목적어와 같을 때는 생략한다.

1) 문장주어와 동일할 때

  I am not ashamed of being poor.

  He is proud of being a scholar.

2) 문장주어와 다를 때

  I insist on his going there.

  I insist on my son going there.

3. 동명사의 시제

동명사의 형태는 단순동명사와 완료동명사로 나뉜다. 단순동명사는 그 시제가 술부의 시제와 같거나 하나 더 나아간 미래의 시제이며, 완료동명사는 술부의 동사보다 하나 앞선 시제이다.

1) 단순동명사

He is proud of being bold.

= He is proud that he is bold.

He was proud of being bold.

= He was proud that he was bold.

He is sure of passing the examination.

= He is sure that he will pass the examination.

2) 완료동명사

I regret having been lazy.

= I regret that I have been(was) lazy.

He regretted having done so.

= He regretted that he had done so.

I never heard of such a thing having been done.

= I never heard that such a thing had been done.

4. 동사에 따른 목적어 형태(동명사와 부정사)

1) 부정사와 동명사 둘 다를 목적어로 취하는 동사

attempt, begin, cease, continue, intend, like, love, omit, start

It continued raining (to rain) all day.

I like taking (to take) a nap after lunch.

I love watching(to watch) TV.

* 목적어가 동명사 또는 부정사일 때 의미가 달라지는 경우

stop + 동명사(~하는 것을 멈추다): I stopped smoking.

stop + 부정사(~하기 위해 멈추다): I stopped to smoke.

remember + 동명사(~한 것을 기억하다): I remember meeting him.

remember + 부정사(~할 것을 기억하고 있다): I remember to meet him.

forget + 동명사(~한 것을 잊어버리다): I forgot posting the letter.

forget + 부정사(~할 것을 잊어버리다): I forgot to post the letter.

try + 동명사(시험 삼아 ~하다): He tried moving the piano.

try + 부정사(~하려고 시도하다, 노력하다): He tried to move the piano.

go on + 동명사(계속해서 ~하다): He went on talking about his life.

go on + 부정사(쉬었다가 다시 계속하다): He went on to talk about his life.

2) 동명사만을 목적어로 취하는 동사

admit, appreciate, avoid, consider, deny, enjoy, escape, e finish, keep, mind, postpone, quit, remind, suggest

You should quit smoking.

Everyone enjoys singing a song.

She finished reading the novel this morning.

3) 부정사만을 목적어로 취하는 동사

agree, appear, ask, choose, decide, demand, desire, expect, hope, learn, manage, plan, pretend, promise, propose, refuse, seem, tend, want, wish

He promised me not to tell a lie.
He decided to study hard.
I expect to be promoted to manager soon.

5. 동명사의 관용적 용법

It is no use ~ing = It is of no use + to 부정사: '~해도 소용없다'
It is no use crying over spilt milk.
    = It is of no use to cry over spilt milk.

It goes without saying that ~: '~은 말할 필요조차 없다'
It goes without saying that honesty is the key to success.

cannot help ~ing = cannot but + 원형: '~하지 않을 수 없다. ~할 수밖에 없다'
I could not help laughing at the funny sight.
    = I could not but laugh at the funny sight.

feel like ~ing: '~하고 싶은 생각이 들다'
I feel like making a trip somewhere.

be busy ~ing: '~하는데 분주하다. ~하느라고 바쁘다'

He was busy preparing for the exam.

go ~ing: ~하러 가다(주로 여가 활동을 언급할 때 쓰인다)

I went fishing yesterday.

look forward to ~ing: '~을 기대하다'

I am looking forward to seeing you again.

Exercise

A. 아래 문장에서 동명사를 확인하고, 그 역할(주어, 보어, 목적어)을 표시하세요.

1. Talking with him is very interesting.
2. The students often avoid answering their teacher's questions.
3. My mother stopped me from making a mistake.
4. Her hobby is gardening.
5. Thanks for inviting me.

B. 아래 문장에서 알맞은 것을 선택하세요.

1. He decided (to buy, buying) the car.
2. All of them don't want (to play, playing) soccer.
3. I don't mind (to study, studying) with him.
4. My brother is busy (to do, doing) his project.
5. We can't help (to laugh, laughing) at his jokes.
6. He promised (to let, letting) me know what the teacher said.
7. Could you show me a (to sleep, sleeping) bag?

Colors

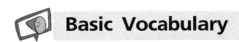

silver	gold
red	orange
yellow	green
blue	purple
pink	gray
brown	white
black	bronze

What color does it stand for?

Charles: I like your yellow sweater.
You look good in yellow.

Andrew: Yellow is my favorite color. Did a singer sing our national anthem?

Charles: Yes he did. Look! There are many national flags behind the stage.

Andrew: All of them are beautiful. Every flag has its own special color.

Charles: The color of the flags stands for the country's identity.

Andrew: What colors does your country stand for?

Charles: I think they are white and blue.

Andrew: White stands for purity and blue stands for peace.

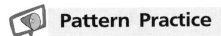

My favorite color is _____.

_____ is the symbol of _____.

A: What color is it?

B: It is _____.

A: What color makes you comfortable?

B: It is _____.

1. When can you pay me back?

2. To whom is Mr. James talking?

3. How long will you stay here?

4. Is there a pay phone around here?

5. Congratulate me! I was promoted to be the vice president!

6. Aren't you in the mood for a horror film?

7. Do you have Jim's number on you?

8. Will you be able to do it?

9. Have you finished taking inventory?

10. Who won the game?

Choosing the correct answer

1. When can you pay me back?

   (A) You don't need to pay the money.

   (B) I'll give you some money on pay day.

   (C) I'm sorry. You're late.

2. To whom is Mr. James talking?

   (A) He is talking about the matter.

   (B) To his client.

   (C) Let's talk to them first.

3. How long will you stay here?

   (A) I'm ten years old.

   (B) The bus will be here in ten minutes.

   (C) About one week.

4. Is there a pay phone around here?

   (A) You have to pay before you make your call.

   (B) Next to the convenience store.

   (C) Make an appointment with my secretary.

5. Congratulate me! I was promoted to be the vice president!

   (A) What? The vice president is coming to my office?

   (B) I'm sorry, the vice president is not in.

   (C) Hey, this calls for a celebration. Let's have a party!

6. Aren't you in the mood for a horror film?

   (A) No way. I hate that stuff.

   (B) Yes, I'd like to go to the film festival.

   (C) No, I have enough rolls of film.

7. Do you have Jim's number on you?

   (A) Yes, let me check my phone book.

   (B) No, his seat number is 45.

   (C) OK. I'll call you at that number.

8. Will you be able to do it?

   (A) Of course. I finished it.

   (B) I am sorry. I can't.

   (C) I don't know him.

9. Have you finished taking inventory?

   (A) Yes, I invented the new system.

   (B) No, I'm only halfway done.

   (C) No, the inventory is in the second drawer.

10. Who won the game?

   (A) I want to win.

   (B) We did. It's one-sided.

   (C) They made the program.

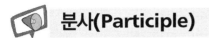 # 분사(Participle)

의미: 동사의 뜻을 그대로 가지고 있으며, 문장에서 다른 품사처럼 쓰인다.

역할: 문장에서 동사적 성질을 갖고, 동사 또는 형용사처럼 쓰인다.

형태: 동사원형 + ing or 동사원형 + ed

종류: 현재분사, 과거분사

* 동사 역할: 진행형, 완료형, 수동태에서 쓰일 때

He is studying English.

The book was written by me.

They have worked for five years.

1. 분사의 의미

1) 현재분사: 진행(~하고 있는),

　　　　　능동 또는 사역(~시키는, ~하게 하는)을 나타냄.

A rolling stone gathers no moss.

People living in the country generally live long.

Look at that falling leaves.

A growing number of young people seek a job.

2) 과거분사: 완료나 상태(~한, ~해버린),
수동(~된, ~당한, ~받은)을 나타냄.

Look at the mountain covered with snow.

A wounded soldier lay bleeding.

The broken computer is mine.

* 의미 비교

It was an exiting game.

An exited spectator starts yelling.

He was exited by the news of the victory

The baseball game was exiting.

The story is interesting.

He was interested in the subject.

It is a surprising event.

I was surprised to hear the news.

His speech was boring

I was bored to hear his speech.

2. 분사의 용법

1) 한정적 용법

(1) 전위 수식: 분사가 단독으로 명사 앞에서 그 명사를 수식한다.

Don't wake up the sleeping child.

Spoken language and written language are two aspects of language.

(2) 후위 수식: 분사가 단독으로 쓰이더라도 대명사를 수식할 때.

Those swimming in the pond are my classmates.

Of those invited, all but Tom came to the party.

분사가 보어, 목적어, 부사(구) 등의 부속어구와 같이 쓰이면 형용사구가 되어 후위 수식한다.

The child sleeping there is Mary.

Once there lived a man named Robin Hood.

2) 서술적 용법

(1) 주격보어로 쓰일 때

He sat reading a novel.

He stood looking at the picture.)

He sat surrounded by his children.

He came in quite exhausted.

(2) 목적격보어로 쓰인다.

I saw him going into the room.

I felt myself watched all the time.

I heard him well spoken of.

I couldn't make myself understood in English.

3. 분사구문

복문(두 개 이상의 절로 만들어진 문장)에서 분사로 시작하는 절에서 사용되며, 사용된 분사는 접속사 + 주어 + 동사가 포함되어 있는 것

1) 때: when, while, as, after

Walking along the street, I met an old friend of mine.

  → While I was walking along the street, I met an old friend of mine.

Left alone, I began to read.

  → When I was left alone, I began to read.

* 다음의 경우에는 being과 having been은 생략되는 것이 보통이다.

(1) 분사구문이 수동태일 경우(과거분사 앞에 놓일 때)

As he was wounded in the legs, he could not walk.

  → (Being) Wounded in the legs, he could not work.

As I had been pleased with the article, I bought it.

  → (Having been) Pleased with the article, I bought it.

(2) 형용사, 명사, 부사, 현재분사 앞에 놓일 때

(Having been) Lazy all his life, he had nothing to offer to his son.

As he is an expert, he knows how to do it.

  → (Being) An expert, he knows how to do it.

(Being) Only a poor student, I hadn't money enough to buy it.

As I was reading a book, he came in.

  → (Being) Reading a book, he came in.

2) 원인, 이유: as, because, since

Having nothing to do, I went to bed.

  → As I had nothing to do, I went to bed.

Not knowing what to do, he just stood and looked.

    → As he did not know what to do, he just stood and looked.

  * 분사구문의 부정: 분사 앞에 not 또는 never를 붙인다.

3) 조건: if

Meeting her, I shall be very glad.

    → If I meet her, I shall be very glad.

Read carelessly, Some books will do more harm than good.

    → If they are read carelessly, some books will do more harm than good.

4) 양보: though, although, even if

Young, she has much experience.

    → Though she is young, she has much experience.

Born of the same parents, they bear no resemblance.

    → Though they were born of the same parents, they bear no resemblance.

5) 부대상황

(1) 동시동작: while, as(~하면서)

Smiling brightly, she shook hands with me.

    → She smiled brightly and shook hands with me.

Raising his hands, he stood up and answered.

    → As he raised his hands, he stood up and answered.

Singing and dancing together, we had a good time.

    → As we sang and danced together, we had a good time.

(2) 연속동작: and + 동사(그리고 ~하다)

We started in the morning, arriving in Seoul at seven.

    → We started in the morning, and arrived in Seoul at seven.

He picked up a stone, throwing it at a dog.

    → He picked up a stone, and threw it at a dog.

4. 분사의 시제

분사는 단순형 분사와 완료형 분사로 나눌 수 있다. 단순형 분사는 주절의 시제와 같은 시제를, 완료형 분사는 주절의 시제보다 하나 앞선 시제를 나타낸다. 즉, 주절의 동사가 현재이면 완료형 분사의 시제는 과거 또는 현재완료이며, 주절의 동사가 과거이면 완료형분사의 시제는 과거완료가 된다.

Living in the country, I am very healthy.

    → As I live in the country, I am very healthy.

Having finished the work, I have much free time now.

    → As I have finished the work, I have much free time now.

Written in plain English, this book is very easy to read.

    → As this book is written in plain English, it is very easy to read.

Scolded, she cried.

    → As she was scolded, she cried.

5. 독립분사구문

분사구문의 의미상의 주어가 주절의 주어와 다를 경우에는 의미상의 주어를 따로 써주어야 한다. 이와 같이 분사구문의 의미상의 주어가 주절의 주어와 다른 분사구문을 독립분사구문이라고 한다.

After the sun had set, we gave up looking for them.

→ The sun having set, we gave up looking for them.

As it was fine, we went for a walk.

→ It being fine, we went for a walk.

We shall start tomorrow, if (the) weather permits.

→ We shall start tomorrow, weather permitting.

Though I admit what you say, my friends still don't believe it.

→ I admitting what you say, my friends still don't believe it.

He was reading a book, and his wife was knitting beside him.

→ He was reading a book, his wife knitting beside him.

Exercise

A. 밑줄 친 분사가 수식하고 있는 것을 확인하세요.

1. The old man <u>sitting</u> on the bench looks tired.
2. The <u>broken</u> computer will be fixed.
3. I couldn't believe the <u>shocking</u> news.
4. All of the <u>invited</u> students enjoyed the show.
5. The meeting <u>scheduled</u> for this evening is canceled.

B. 문장에 알맞은 형태를 고르세요.

1. She left the door (unlocking, unlocked).
2. The (retiring, retired) man visited the company.
3. They found the (losing, lost) child in the park.
4. The game was very (exciting, excited).
5. The building (painting, painted) green is a shopping center.

C. 밑줄 친 분사를 풀어쓰세요.

1. <u>Seeing</u> me, he ran away.
2. <u>Finishing</u> the homework, she takes a nap.
3. <u>Being</u> sick, Tom didn't attend the meeting.
4. <u>Following</u> this road, you will find the police station.
5. <u>Being</u> sick, I finished the project.

Animals

fox	wolf	tiger
leopard	lion	hyena
elephant	deer	squirrel
rabbit	bat	giraffe
donkey	horse	pony
buffalo	camel	cow
pig	kangaroo	zebra
bear	panda	monkey
chimpanzee	gorilla	hamster

Look at the monkey!

Linda: Look at the monkeys!

Andrew: All of them look sleepy.

Linda: Shall we give them bananas into the cage?

Andrew: No, don't do that. It will hurt them. Let's go to see buffaloes.

Linda: Good. Where are they?

Andrew: They will be a wild place over there.

Linda: Wow! They look big and wild. I have never seen them before.

Andrew: I saw them in Yellow Stone national park. There were many buffaloes in the field without guarding.

Linda: Did you! The park is the first national park in USA. Is it a nice place to visit?

Andrew: Yes. The park is huge. Many travellers usually stay there several days to see the park.

I like _____ because _____.

I don't like _____ because _____.

A: What is the biggest animal in the world?

B: I think it is the _____.

A: What kinds of animals are there in the zoo?

B: There are _____ _____ _____ in the zoo.

1. Where's my ring?

2. What does it look like?

3. Why don't you buy it?

4. Are you sure it has no problem?

5. You've gone too far! Take back your words!

6. Didn't you have lunch?

7. Do you know how to operate this program?

8. Would you like something to drink?

9. Have you renewed your driver's license?

10. What's your boss like?

Choosing the correct answer

1. Where's my ring?

   (A) On third avenue.

   (B) On the desk.

   (C) On Monday.

2. What does it look like?

   (A) I like it very much.

   (B) It is small and round.

   (C) It looks at the sky.

3. Why don't you buy it?

   (A) I don't have enough money for it.

   (B) Money is good for him.

   (C) There are many boats at the bay.

4. Are you sure it has no problem?

   (A) Yes, she's a problem child.

   (B) Yes, don't worry about it.

   (C) Yes, I'm sure you're right.

5. You've gone too far! Take back your words!

   (A) I'm sorry. I fully apologize.

   (B) Sure! I give you my word.

   (C) I'm already on the highway.

6. Didn't you have lunch?

   (A) No, I skipped it because I was tied up with work.

   (B) Yes, I had a good time.

   (C) Yes, the party was crowded with people.

7. Do you know how to operate this program?

   (A) Yes, I did it.

   (B) Yes, the program will be on TV at 6.

   (C) No, I'm computer-illiterate.

8. Would you like something to drink?

   (A) What do you have?

   (B) What can I do for you?

   (C) What kind of juice?

9. Have you renewed your driver's license?

   (A) No, but I'll do that sometime this weekend.

   (B) Thank you for the tip.

   (C) Not yet. But they'll be delivered on Thursday.

10. What's your boss like?

   (A) He is so critical.

   (B) No, he doesn't likes it.

   (C) He has no interest in it.

수동태(Passive)

의미: 의사 전달에 있어 문장주어의 관점에 따른 문장표현 방법으로, 일반적으로 많은 문장들은 능동문으로 사용되고 있으나, 때때로 주어가 동작이나, 행위를 받는 문장을 사용할 때가 있다. 이를 수동태 문장이라 한다.

역할: 주어가 동작을 받는 문장으로서 각종 보고서나 전달문의 문장으로 사용되고, 때때로 강조를 하고자 할 때 사용한다.

일반구조: 주어 + be동사 + 과거분사 + by 목적어

1. 태의 전환

능동태와 수동태: 능동태는 동작을 하는 쪽에, 수동태는 동작을 받는 쪽에 중점

1) 능동태를 수동태로 바꿀 때

(1) 능동태의 목적어가 수동태의 주어가 된다.
(2) 능동태의 동사는 be + 과거분사의 형태로 바뀐다.
(3) 능동태의 주어는 by + 목적격의 형태로 부사구를 이룬다.

He wrote this letter.

→ This letter was written by him.

All the people in the world admire Kennedy.

→ Kennedy is admired by all the people in the world.

* 주의: 자동사는 수동태가 될 수 없다.

lie, sit, rise, die, arrive, work, wait, belong, consist, (dis)appear, exist, occur, happen, originate

The cost of transportation has been risen with the price of gasoline.(×)

* 주의: 타동사이지만 수동태로 전환할 수 없는 동사

resemble, have, meet, lack, escape, belong to, let.

He resembles his father.

　　→ His father is resembled by him.(×)

He escaped death.

　　→ Death was escaped by him.(×)

2. 수동태의 시제: 수동태의 be동사는 능동태 동사의 시제와 일치한다.

The hotel was built (by people) in 1994.

	현재	과거	미래
단순형	is built	was built	will be built
완료형	has been built	had been built	will have been built
진행형	is being built	was being built	(will be being built)

* 주의: 조동사가 있을 경우에 조동사는 그대로 둔다. 그러나 will, shall은 인칭에 맞게 바꾸어 주어야 한다.

You must read the book.

　　→ The book must be read by you.

Jack can build the house.

　　→ The house can be built by Jack.

3. 주의할 수동태

1) 4형식의 수동태: 능동태 4형식에 있는 직접목적어와 간접목적어를 주어로 선택 할 수 있다.

Henry gave me these books.

    → I was given these books by Henry.

       These books were given me by Henry.

       These books were given to me by Henry.

He asked me the question.

    → I was asked the question by him.

       The question was asked me by him.

       The question was asked of me by him.

* 직접목적어를 주어로 하여 전치사를 수반할 때, 직접목적어를 주어로 하면 간접목적어는 보류목적어(Retained Object)가 된다. 이 때 보류목적어 앞에는 to, for, of 등의 전치사가 놓인다.

(send, tell, lend, give : to/make, buy : for/ask, require, inquire : of)

* 주의: make, buy, write, sing, send, pass, get, bring 등의 수여동사는 직접목적어만 수동태의 주어가 될 수 있다.

I wrote him a letter. → A letter was written him by me.(O)

                  He was written a letter by me.(×)

She sang me a song. → A song was sung me by her.(O)

                 I was sung a song by her.(×)

* 주의: spare, save, envy, kiss, answer 등의 수여동사는 간접목적어만 수동
태의 주어가 될 수 있다.

They envied him his luck.

→ He was envied his luck by them.(O)

His luck was envied him by them.(×)

He kissed her good night.

→ She was kissed good night by him.

2) 능동태 5형식을 수동태로 고치면 2형식이 된다.

이 때 막연한 일반인을 나타내는 we, you, one, they, people, somebody, someone 등은 수동태에서 생략되는 경우가 많다.

I painted the gate green. → The gate was painted green by me.

They elected Kennedy President. → Kennedy was elected President.

(by them)

They elected him chairman. → He was elected chairman. (by them)

3) 보어가 원형부정사인 수동태: 술부동사가 지각동사 또는 사역동사일 경우, 원형부정
사는 수동태에서 'to 부정사'로 바뀐다.

He made me do it.

→ I was made to do it by him.

We saw him enter the room.

→ He was seen to enter the room. (by us)

We heard him sing.

→ He was heard to sing by us.

4. 의문문의 수동태

1) 의문사가 없는 의문문

Did you plant this tree?
    평서문 → You planted this tree.
    수동태 → This tree was planted by you.
    의문문 → Was this tree planted by you?

2) 의문사가 있는 의문문

What did he do?
    평서문 → He did what. (비문장)
    수동태 → What was done by him. (비문장)
    의문문 → What was done by him?

5. 수동태가 많이 쓰이는 경우

1) 능동태의 주어가 분명치 않을 때

He was killed in the war.
The continent was discovered about 300 years ago.

2) 능동태의 주어가 막연한 일반인을 나타낼 때

Spanish is spoken in Mexico, too.
The rule was seldom observed.

3) 능동태의 주어보다 수동태의 주어에 더 관심이 클 때

The child was run over by a car.
Mr. Reagan was elected President again.
The bed was not slept in.

4) 수동태의 의미가 거의 없이 자동사로 느껴지는 경우

He was drowned while swimming in this river.
Her eyes were drowned in tears.
He was suddenly taken ill.
My University is located on the hill.
He was born in 1970.
He is ashamed of what he did.

6. 수동태에서 'by' 이외의 전치사를 쓰는 경우

1) 'at'을 쓰는 동사: surprise, shock

I am surprised at the news.

2) 'in'을 쓰는 동사: interest

I am interested in the movie.

3) 'with'을 쓰는 동사: cover, satisfy, please

I am satisfied with the result.

Exercise

A.아래 문장이 능동태문장인지, 수동태 문장인지 확인하세요.

1. Tom bought Jane a ring.
2. The shopping mall will be opened soon.
3. He has waited his children for two hours.
4. Many students has respected the teacher.
5. The book was published.

B. 아래 문장을 수동태로 바꾸세요.

1. They broke the window yesterday.
2. Shakespeare wrote Hamlet.
3. The policeman arrested the thief.
4. I will finish the project.
5. He gave me a gift.

C. 빈 칸에 알맞은 전치사를 쓰세요.

1. I am interested (   ) English.
2. My father satisfied (   ) his work.
3. The ground is covered (   ) snow.
4. He was surprised (   ) the news.

Clothing

Shirt	blouse
sweater	jacket
vest	bra
pants	shorts
skirt	underpants
running shorts	uniform
suit	dress
nightgown	bathrobe
coat	raincoat
trench coat	pajamas

How about this green T-shirt?

Robert: I can't find my blue T-shirt?

Olivia: Did you check in the closet?

Robert: I already looked there. It will be very fit for me today.

Olivia: How about this green T-shirt? It will be good for you.

Robert: Ok, I will take it. I don't have enough time. We had better hurry up.

Olivia: Many people will participate the campaign. All of them will wear casual clothes.

Robert: We have to bring raincoats. It will be raining at the afternoon.

Olivia: I will also bring a jacket.

Could you show me new _____?

I will take the _____.

A: I am looking for _____.

B: You can find _____ over there.

A: Where did you buy _____?

B: I bought _____ at Lotte store.

1. When do you need that report?

2. Who will be sent to the meeting?

3. How did you like the meeting?

4. Is he a friend of yours?

5. I'm hungry. Let's have a bite to eat!

6. Can't you make a little less noise?

7. Does your boss often go to play golf?

8. Will the movie be over on time?

9. Have you seen my cellphone anywhere?

10. Did you hear Jane resigned yesterday?

Choosing the correct answer

1. When do you need that report?

   (A) At the end of this month.

   (B) I need the blue one.

   (C) On Friday, last week.

2. Who will be sent to the meeting?

   (A) The meeting is on Wednesday.

   (B) How about Jim?

   (C) Ken will be fired.

3. How did you like the meeting?

   (A) I don't like meat.

   (B) It's five today.

   (C) It was very useful.

4. Is he a friend of yours?

   (A) No, I don't want to see.

   (B) Yes, I agree with your opinion.

   (C) No, I hardly know him.

5. I'm hungry. Let's have a bite to eat!

   (A) I've got lots of mosquito bites as well.

   (B) Good idea! How about going for a salad?

   (C) I can't eat any kind of meat.

6. Can't you make a little less noise?

    (A) Sorry, I didn't mean to disturb you.

    (B) Sure. What time?

    (C) You need to practice a little more.

7. Does your boss often go to play golf?

    (A) Once in a blue moon. He usually goes to play tennis.

    (B) That's too bad the company let him go.

    (C) I want to learn how to play golf.

8. Will the movie be over on time?

    (A) I don't think so.

    (B) It's time to go.

    (C) Time cannot wait for us.

9. Have you seen my cellphone anywhere?

    (A) I haven't seen him for weeks.

    (B) Did you check your car?

    (C) I know you're good at speaking.

10. Did you hear Jane resigned yesterday?

    (A) No. What makes her do that?

    (B) Yes. I heard she bought it yesterday.

    (C) Yes. I saw her meeting her boyfriend.

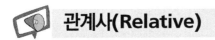 **관계사(Relative)**

의미: 두 문장을 하나로 연결하지만, 순수 접속사와 달리 선행사가 있다.

역할: 접속사 + 명사 혹은 부사 역할

종류: 관계대명사, 관계부사

1. 관계대명사

주격	소유격	목적격	선행사
who	whose	whom	사람
which	whose/of which	which	사물/동물
that	-	that	사람/사물/동물
what	-	what	(선행사 포함)

1) Who

(1) 주격

He is the man. + He saved the child.

→ He is the man who saved the child.

I employed a man. + He I thought was honest.

→ I employed a man who I thought was honest.

(2) 소유격

This is the gentleman. + His pulse has been stolen.

→ This is the gentleman whose purse has been stolen.

A child is called an orphan. + His parents are dead.

→ A child whose parents are dead is called an orphan.

(3) 목적격

He is the man. + She saved him.

→ He is the man whom she saved.

I employed a man. + I thought him to be honest.

→ I employed a man whom I thought to be honest.

2) Which

(1) 주격

I have a book. + It is very interesting.

→ I have a book which is very interesting.

(2) 목적격

This is the book. + I bought it yesterday.

→ This is the book which I bought yesterday.

(3) 소유격: whose, of which

The house is my uncle's. + Its roof is red.

→ The house whose roof is red is my uncle's.

→ The house of which the roof is red is my uncle's.

3) That

(1) 선행사에 최상급, 서수, the only, the very, the last, the first 등과 같은 강한 한정 어구가 붙을 때나, 선행사가 부정형용사(any, no, all, some, little, few,

much)에 의해 수식을 받을 때 관계대명사 who 또는 which 보다 that을 주로 쓴다.

This is the best movie that I have ever seen.

He is the only poet that I know well.

There is no man that doesn't love his own country.

(2) 선행사가 '사람 + 동물', '사람 + 사물'일 때.

Look at the boy and his dog that are running over there.

The driver and the car that fell into the river have not been found.

4) What

선행사를 포함하고 있기 때문에 what = that which, the thing which, all that 등으로 바꿀 수 있다.

(1) 주어절: What I want is your advice. (what = That which)

(2) 보어절: I am not what I used to be. (what = the man that)

(3) 목적어절: I will do what I can. (what = all that)

5) 관계대명사의 두 용법(' , '의 유무에 따라 구분)

(1) 제한적 용법

He had two sons who became doctors.

She is the first love that I loved.

(2) 계속적 용법: 관계대명사가 계속적 용법으로 쓰일 때, 문장의 내용에 따라 접속사 + 대명사(and, but, for, though + 대명사)로 바꾸어 쓸 수 있다.

He had two sons, who became doctors. (who = and they)

We trust him, who is very honest. (who = for he)

This book, which is old, is of great value to me. (which = though it)

* 관계대명사 what와 that은 계속적 용법이 없다.

I cannot understand, what he says.(×)

He has a horse, that runs very fast.(×)

6) 관계대명사의 생략(목적격 관계대명사)

(1) 동사의 목적어가 될 때

This is the man (whom) I like best.

The movie (which) I saw yesterday was interesting.

He is the only poet (that) I know well.

(2) 전치사의 목적어가 될 때

This is the man (whom) you spoke of the other day.

This is the hotel (which) we stopped at last time.

2. 관계부사

선행사를 가지면서, 접속사와 부사의 구실을 한다. 이 때 선행사 시간(때), 장소, 이유, 방법을 나타내는 명사이다. 관계부사는 전치사 + which로 바꾸어 쓸 수 있다.

종류: when, where, why, how

1) when: 선행사가 time, day, occasion, season 등의 '때'를 나타낼 때 쓰인다. 이
때 when은 at, in, on, during + which로 바꾸어 쓸 수 있다.

I don't know the time. + It happened then.
→ I don't know the time when it happened. (when = at which)

2) where: 선행사가 place, house, town, village 등의 '장소'를 나타낼 때 쓰인다.
이 때 where는 in, at, to + which로 바꾸어 쓸 수 있다.

This is the village. + I was born there.
→ This is the village where I was born. (where = in which)

3) why: 선행사가 reason일 때 쓰인다. why는 for + which로 바꾸어 쓸 수 있다.

Tell me the reason. + You did not come for that reason.
→ Tell me the reason why you did not come. (why = for which)

4) how: 방법을 나타내며, 선행사 없이 쓰인다.

This is the way. + It happened in that way.
→ This is (the way) how it happened.
→ This is the way in which it happened.

3. 복합관계사

1) 복합관계대명사

복합관계대명사는 관계대명사 + ever의 형태로서, 자체에 선행사를 포함하고 있으며 (선행사 + 관계대명사), 명사절 또는 부사절로 쓰인다.

종류: whoever, whomever, whosever, whichever, whatever

(1) 명사절을 유도할 때
Whoever comes is welcome. (= Anyone who: ~하는 사람은 누구나)
Give it to whomever you like. (= anyone whom)
Return it whosever address is on it. (= anyone whose)
You may take whichever you like. (= anything that: ~하는 것은 어느 것이나)
I will give you whatever you need. (= anything that: ~하는 것은 무엇이나)

(2) 양보의 부사절을 유도할 때: '누가/누구를/어떤 것을/무엇을 ~한다 할지라도'
Whoever may break this law, he will be punished. (= No matter who)
Whomever you may love, he will desert you. (= No matter whom)
Whichever you may choose, you will be interested in it. (= No matter which)
Whatever happens, I will go. (= No matter what)

2) 복합관계부사

선행사를 자체에 포함하고 있으며 부사절을 유도한다.

종류: wherever, whenever, however

(1) wherever 장소의 부사절: ~하는 곳은 어디든지

　　　　　양보의 부사절: ~로(에) …할지라도

　You may go wherever you like. (= at any place where)

　Wherever she is, I will find her. (= No matter where)

(2) whenever 시간의 부사절: ~할 때는 언제나

　　　　　양보의 부사절: 언제 ~할지라도

　You may come whenever you like. (= at any time that)

　Whenever you may call on me, you will find me at my desk. (= No matter when)

(3) however 양보의 부사절: 아무리 ~할지라도

　However hard you may try, you cannot do it in a week. (= No matter how)

　However rich a man may be, he should not be idle. (= No matter how)

Exercise

A. 아래 문장에서 관계사와 선행사에 밑줄을 치세요.

1. I know him who lives in Denver.
2. This is the phone which I bought yesterday.
3. He met a man whose son is a singer.
4. This is the only pen that I have.
5. I don't know the time when the shop is open.

B. 두 개의 문장을 하나로 합치세요.

1. This is the book. I want to buy it.
2. This is the town. I was born there.
3. I bought a phone. Its screen is wide.
4. He likes the computer. His father bought him it.
5. I know a man. He works for the company.

C. 빈칸에 알맞은 관계사를 써 넣으세요.

1. Do you know the man (   ) is watching the game?
2. I have a girl friend (   ) father is a professor.
3. I gave my son all the money (   ) I had.
4. Sunday is the day (   ) we go to church.
5. Do you know the reason (   ) he is so happy?

Musical Instruments

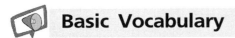

flute	clarinet	oboe
recorder	saxophone	
trumpet	trombone	tuba
violin	viola	cello
guitar	ukulele	mandolin
harp		
drum	cymbals	xylophone
piano	organ	
accordion	harmonica	

My sister is a fan of the band.

Charles: Do you hear about the famous band concert?

Andrew: I didn't. I think the band is great.
My sister is a fan of the band.

Charles: I am going to buy tickets for me and my wife.
Tickets are usually cheaper if we get them in advance.

Andrew: I will ask if my sister want to or not. She used
to play violin and drum. But, she doesn't play any
musical instrument these days. She may be too busy.

Charles: If you want to, you can get tickets at the door.

Andrew: I hope the concert will be successful.

I can play the _____.

The _____ sound is fantastic!

A: Do you play a musical instrument?

B: Yes. I play the _____.

A: What is the name of the _____?

B: It is _____.

1. Where did you get the news?

2. What do you think about the game?

3. Why are you so angry?

4. Was 'KK Project' the first thing you planned?

5. Be sure to back up all the files in this folder.

6. Don't you have this coat in a smaller size?

7. Did you have a chance to check out the annual report?

8. Would you like a receipt?

9. Have the board members settled their differences?

10. How big is the new printer?

Choosing the correct answer

1. Where did you get the news?

   (A) I got an e-mail yesterday.

   (B) The news is very interesting.

   (C) You can see the computer.

2. What do you think about the game?

   (A) I can't decide yet.

   (B) It's very exciting.

   (C) I should have done it.

3. Why are you so angry?

   (A) I can speak English.

   (B) He deceived me again.

   (C) It looks like a triangle.

4. Was 'KK Project' the first thing you planned?

   (A) Yes, I am planning to improve the first project.

   (B) Yes, that's the second project.

   (C) No, KK project was Mr. Brown's.

5. Be sure to back up all the files in this folder.

   (A) I've already saved them in a USB flash drive.

   (B) OK. I'll send you the data.

   (C) Yes. I bought this file folder yesterday.

6. Don't you have this coat in a smaller size?

   (A) No, that's the smallest.

   (B) No, we don't have a larger size.

   (C) No, but you are a very small man.

7. Did you have a chance to check out the annual report?

   (A) No, we'll check in when the manager comes.

   (B) Not yet. Has the report been issued already?

   (C) Yes, all the copies are checked out.

8. Would you like a receipt?

   (A) Yes, please. I'll need one for tax purposes.

   (B) No thanks. I'll pay in cash.

   (C) The recipe is hard to understand.

9. Have the board members settled their differences?

   (A) No. They are still in the meeting room.

   (B) Yes. They found the defendant guilty.

   (C) Yes. The meeting is held every third week.

10. How big is the new printer?

    (A) Yes, I want a big printer.

    (B) It's a little smaller than the old one.

    (C) It looks like a space ship.

의미: 영어에서는 주어에 따라서 동사가 단수형인가 복수형인가를 선택하여야
한다.

1. 주어와 동사의 일치

1) 주어의 단수와 복수

My friend lives in Boston.
My brother and sister live in Boston.

2) 명사구나 절이 주어가 되는 경우: 단수로 받는다.

Growing flowers is her hobby. (동명사구)
To live long is the desire of man. (부정사구)
Whether he will agree with me is doubtful. (명사절)

3) and로 연결되는 경우

and로 연결되는 두 개 이상의 명사가 별개의 사람이나 사물이면 복수로, 동일한
사람이나 사물이면 단수로 취급한다.

John and Jim are roommates this semester.

A teacher and scientist is supposed to come.

4) 형용사 every와 each ⇒ 단수를 수식하고, 단수 취급한다.

Every boy and girl is taught to read and write.
Every man, woman, and child needs love.
Each book and magazine is listed in the card catalog.

2. 수량 표시

1) each[one/every one] of + 복수명사 ⇒ 단수 취급

Every one of my friends is here.
One of the most famous films is Gone with the Wind.
Each of the boys has his own desk.

2) a number of + 복수명사 ⇒ 복수 취급
the number of + 복수명사 ⇒ 단수 취급

A number of students were late for class. (a number of = many)
The number of students in the class is fifteen. (~의 숫자)

3) many a + 단수명사 ⇒ 단수 취급

Many a soldier was killed at the field.

3. 수의 일치

1) 'there'로 유도되는 구문의 동사는 주어와 일치시킨다.

There are twenty students in my class.
There's a fly in the room.

2) 회사[단체] 이름, 지명, 학문 명, 유희 등은 단수로 받는다.

Sears is a department store.
Physics is easy for her.
Billiards is usually played by two persons.

3) 시간, 거리, 가격의 표현이 하나의 의미로 쓰일 경우 단수 취급한다.

Eight hours of sleep is enough.
Ten years is a long time to wait.
Five thousand miles is too far to travel.
Ten dollars is too much to pay.

4) 수식 표현은 단수 취급한다.

Two and two[Two plus two] is/equals four.
Five times five is twenty five.
Ten minus five leaves/equals five.
Fifteen divided by three is five

5) 나라 이름이나 그 나라 언어를 나타낼 때: 단수
그 나라 사람들을 나타낼 때: 복수

English is spoken in many countries.

Chinese is his native language.

The English drink tea.

The Chinese have an interesting history.

The Americans are a passionate people.

The Koreans are a peace-loving people.

6) the + 형용사: 복수보통명사

The rich get richer. (= rich people)

The poor have many problems. (= poor people)

the young(젊은 사람들)/the dead(죽은 사람들)

7) 상관 접속사의 일치

(1) either A or B/neither A nor B/A or B ⇒ B에 일치(B가 주어)
   John or I am to blame.

(2) not only A but also B ⇒ B/A as well as B ⇒ A에 일치
   James, as well as his friends, was injured in the accident.

(3) both A and B ⇒ 복수 취급
   Both brother and sister are dead.

8) 집합명사(단일성 강조) ⇒ 단수 취급/군집명사(개별성 강조) ⇒ 복수 취급

My family is large.

All my family are early risers.

The audience was a large one.

The audience were all deeply moved.

9) 항상 복수 취급하는 명사

(1) police, peasantry, clergy, nobility: 정관사와 같이 쓰인다.

The police are on the murderer's track.

The clergy are all kindness to the poor.

(2) people, cattle, poultry: 부정관사도 못 붙이고 복수형으로 쓰이지도 않는다.

Those people are from Canada.

Cattle feed on grass.

10) 형식은 복수이지만, 하나의 단위로 취급해서 단수로 받는다.

Ten years is a long time to wait.

A hundred miles is a long distance.

Five hundred dollars a month is a small sum to him.

11) It is ~ that 강조 구문에서는 강조되는 부분과 일치

It is you that are to blame.

It is I who am fit to do this work.

Exercise

A. 문장에 알맞은 형태를 고르세요.

1. The pen on the desk (is, are) mine.

2. Tom and Bill (live, lives) together in the house.

3. Many a soldier (was, were) killed at the war.

4. There (is, are) many people at the room.

5. Either you or I (am, are) supposed to attend the meeting.

6. My family (is, are) all very well.

7. Every boy and every girl in the room (watch, watches) TV

8. The doctor and artist (is, are) my friend.

9. Each of them (is, are) happy.

10. Mathematics (is, are) my favorite subject.

11. Not only she but also I (like, likes) the teacher.

12. Ten dollars (is, are) too much to pay.

Irregular Verbs
Reading Numbers

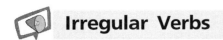

Irregular Verbs

원형	과거	과거분사
awake	awoke	awoken
be	was/were	been
beat	beat	beaten
become	became	become
begin	began	begun
bend	bent	bent
bite	bit	bitten
break	broke	broken
bring	brought	brought
build	built	built
burn	burned/burnt	burned/burnt
buy	bought	bought
catch	caught	caught
choose	chose	chosen
come	came	come
cut	cut	cut
deal	dealt	dealt
dive	dived/dove	dived/drove
do	did	done
draw	drew	drawn
dream	dreamed/dreamt	dreamed/dreamt
drink	drank	drunk
drive	drove	driven
eat	ate	eaten
fall	fell	fallen
feel	felt	felt
fight	fought	fought
fly	flew	flown

원형	과거	과거분사
find	found	found
forget	forgot	forgotten
freeze	froze	frozen
get	got	got/gotten
give	gave	given
go	went	gone
grow	grew	grown
hang	hung	hung
have	had	had
hear	heard	heard
hide	hid	hidden
hit	hit	hit
hold	held	held
hurt	hurt	hurt
keep	kept	kept
know	knew	known
lead	led	led
leave	left	left
lend	lent	lent
let	let	let
lose	lost	lost
make	made	made
meet	met	met
pay	paid	paid
put	put	put
read	read	read
ring	rang	rung
rise	rose	risen
run	ran	run
say	said	said
see	saw	seen

원형	과거	과거분사
seek	sought	sought
sell	sold	sold
send	sent	sent
shake	shook	shaken
shine	shone	shone
shoot	shot	shot
show	showed	shown
shut	shut	shut
sing	sang	sung
sit	sat	sat
sleep	slept	slept
speak	spoke	spoken
spend	spent	spent
stand	stood	stood
steal	stole	stolen
strike	struck	struck
swim	swam	swum
take	took	taken
teach	taught	taught
tell	told	told
think	thought	thought
throw	threw	thrown
wake	woke/waked	woken/waked
wear	wore	worn
win	won	won
write	wrote	written

Reading Numbers

기 수		서 수	
1	one	1st	first
2	two	2nd	second
3	three	3rd	third
4	four	4th	fourth
5	five	5th	fifth
6	six	6th	sixth
7	seven	7th	seventh
8	eight	8th	eighth
9	nine	9th	ninth
10	ten	10th	tenth
11	eleven	11th	eleventh
12	twelve	12th	twelfth
13	thirteen	13th	thirteenth
14	fourteen	14th	fourteenth
15	fifteen	15th	fifteenth
16	sixteen	16th	sixteenth
17	seventeen	17th	seventeenth
18	eighteen	18th	eighteenth
19	nineteen	19th	nineteenth
20	twenty	20th	twentieth
21	twenty-one	21th	twentieth-first
30	thirty	30th	thirtieth
40	forty	40th	fortieth
50	fifty	50th	fiftieth
60	sixty	60th	sixtieth
70	seventy	70th	seventieth
80	eighty	80th	eightieth

기 수		서 수	
90	ninety	90th	ninetieth
100	one hundred		
10,000	ten thousand		
100,000	one hundred thousand		
1,000,000	one million		

Lesson 1   문장의 구조

A. 밑줄 친 단어의 품사를 구분하세요.

1. I forgot to book a <u>ticket</u> for the movie. **(명사)**
2. I am going to meet him <u>at</u> the coffee shop. **(전치사)**
3. Mary <u>and</u> Tom look very happy. **(접속사)**
4. He showed her an <u>expensive</u> computer. **(형용사)**
5. English is not <u>so</u> easy for me. **(부사)**
6. The man invited <u>my</u> sister yesterday. **(대명사)**

B. 아래 문장에서 밑줄 친 동사를 자동사와 타동사로 구분하세요.

1. He <u>smiles</u> at me. **(자동사)**
2. We <u>made</u> a reservation. **(타동사)**
3. They <u>went</u> to the park in the morning. **(자동사)**
4. I <u>found</u> the book difficult. **(타동사)**
5. They don't <u>want</u> to take a bus. **(타동사)**

C. 아래 문장의 몇 형식 문장인지 구분하세요.

1. The beautiful bird is singing on the tree. **(1형식)**
2. I thought it a dog. **(5형식)**
3. The man killed himself on Monday. **(3형식)**
4. Seoul is the capital of Korea. **(2형식)**
5. Could you lend me your pen? **(3형식)**

Lesson 2 　문장의 종류

A. 아래 문장의 종류를 구분하세요.

평서문, 의문문, 명령문, 감탄문

1. What a kind man he is!　　　　　　(감탄문)
2. Did you meet him yesterday?　　　(의문문)
3. Let him go.　　　　　　　　　　　(명령문)
4. Is she a teacher?　　　　　　　　(의문문)
5. The program is very useful.　　　(평서문)

B. 아래문장들을 부정문으로 만드세요.

1. My uncle <u>was</u> very diligent.
　　　　　　　was not
2. My sister <u>watched</u> the TV show yesterday.
　　　　　　　did not watch
3. They <u>paint</u> the roof white.
　　　　　　do not paint
4. William <u>sent</u> Linda the jewelry box.
　　　　　　　did not send
5. I <u>can</u> do it.
　　can not

C. 아래문장들을 의문문으로 만드세요.

1. He is interested in politics.
　　→ **Is he interested in politics?**
2. Susan is from America.
　　→ **Is Susan from America?**
3. She likes to talk on the phone.
　　→ **Does she like to talk on the phone?**
4. Birds sing in the forest.
　　→ **Do birds sing in the forest?**
5. She will do her best tomorrow.
　　→ **Will she do her best tomorrow?**

Lesson 3   명사

A. 아래 문장에서 명사에 밑줄을 치고, 그 종류(보통, 집합, 물질, 추상, 고유)를 쓰세요.

1. The boy wants to be a good <u>doctor</u>.   (보통)
2. He ordered a cup of <u>coffee</u>.   (물질)
3. The <u>audience</u> have to pay extra <u>money</u> for the concert. (물질)
4. There are many people in <u>Seoul</u>.   (고유)
5. <u>Honesty</u> is very important.   (추상)

Lesson 4 대명사

A. 괄호 안에 알맞은 인칭대명사를 써 넣으세요.

1. This question is very difficult for (목적격 대명사; me, …).
2. This pen is (소유대명사; mine, …).
3. She sent (목적격; me, …) a letter.
4. (I, you, we, they) work for Samsung.
5. The man asked me (소유격; my, …) address.

B. 괄호 안에 알맞은 대명사를 써 넣으세요.

1. The girl showed me a red sweater, but I don't like (it).
2. This dog is stronger than (목적격; me, …).
3. They were proud of (목적격; me, …) for winning the game.
4. He said the bag was (소유대명사; mine, …).
5. My mother bought me blue neck ties, and I really like (it).
6. If you need a pen, I will give (one) to you.

C. 아래 문장에서 밑줄 친 "it"의 쓰임을 구분하세요.

1. It is snowing outside.   (비 인칭 주어)
2. How far is it from here to the mall.   (비 인칭 주어)
3. Tom bought a car and he drove it to the school. (a car)
4. How far is it from here to the mall.   (비 인칭 주어)
5. I tried to open the box, but it was impossible. (the box)
6. It is already five.   (비 인칭 주어)

Lesson 5 동사/ 조동사

동사

A. 밑줄 친 동사의 종류를 구분하세요. (be동사, 조동사, 일반동사)

1. He <u>lives</u> in Seoul.   (일반동사)
2. I <u>believe</u> you made a mistake.   (일반동사)
3. The man <u>became</u> a famous artist.   (일반동사)
4. The foreigner <u>can</u> speak Korean.   (조동사)
5. She has <u>finished</u> her project.   (일반동사)
6. Edward <u>was</u> a computer programer.   (be동사)

B. 밑줄 친 동사의 과거형을 쓰세요.

1. I <u>have</u> a lot of books.   (had)
2. She <u>writes</u> Harry Potter.   (wrote)
3. They <u>think</u> he is a doctor.   (thought)
4. Many people <u>want</u> to see the game.   (wanted)
5. The player <u>hit</u> the ball.   (hit)
6. I <u>read</u> a history novel.   (read)

C. 밑줄 친 동사의 시제를 구분하세요.

1. <u>Have</u> you ever been to America?   (현재완료)
2. John <u>is staying</u> in Seoul.   (현재진행)
3. She could not sleep well, because she <u>had had</u> much tea.   (과거완료)
4. My brother <u>will be</u> there about 2:30.   (미래)
5. The teacher <u>has been waiting</u> for his son.   (현재완료진행)

조동사

A. 아래 문장에서 알맞은 것을 고르세요.

1. Eliot (could, **must**) be on vacation this week.
2. He (might, **have to**) meet me at the theater.
3. The boy (**can**, could) attend the English class in the evening.

4. You (could, **should**) do obey your parents.
5. They insist that he (**should**, will) be sent there.
6. (**May**, Must) I borrow your pen?
7. (**Can**, Will) I ask you a question?
8. (May, **Shall**) we dance?
9. (**Would**, Should) you help me?
10. (**Could**, May) you be quite, please.

Lesson 6   관사

A. 밑줄 친 단어 앞에 관사가 필요하면 써 넣으세요.

1. Dog is **a faithful** animal.
2. I need to **a teacher** to help me.
3. I think she is **a music** dancer.
4. **Water** is very important.
5. One of my friends lives in **Seoul**.
6. We should know **life** is not so long.

B. 밑줄 친 부정관사의 의미를 보기에서 찾아 쓰세요.

보기) one, per, some, a certain

1. They talked about <u>a</u> movie.   **(a certain)**
2. There is <u>an</u> apple on the table.   **(one)**
3. My son usually drink two glasses of milk <u>a</u> day.   **(per)**

C. 빈 칸에 알맞은 관사를 써 넣으세요.

1. (**The/a**) caw is a useful animal
2. I don't have (**a**) driver's license.
3. Yesterday, I bought a USB, but I lost (**the**) USB.
4. Please, open (**the**) door.
5. (**The**) sun rises in the east.
6. He caught me by (**the**) hand.

Lesson 7 형용사

A. 밑줄 친 형용사가 꾸며주는 명사를 고르세요.

1. I was late at the meeting because of <u>heavy</u> **traffic**.
2. **Something** <u>spicy</u> was put into her soup.
3. There is a ugly <u>broken</u> **car** on the street.
4. I met **somebody** <u>famous</u> at the mall.
5. My <u>favorite</u> **sport** is baseball.

B. 밑줄 친 형용사가 설명해 주고 있는 단어(명사 또는 대명사) 또는 구를 고르세요.

1. **The city** is <u>fantastic</u>.
2. My mother always made **me** <u>happy</u>.
3. I know **he** is very <u>smart</u>.
4. I think they believed **him** <u>honest</u>.

C. 문장에 알맞은 것을 고르세요.

1. I have (a few, **a little**) breakfast in the morning.
2. He spent (**many**, much) days doing his project.
3. There is (many, **much**) snow in this winter.
4. How (**many**, much) pictures did you take in USA.
5. I don't have (a few, **a little**) knowledge about it.
6. The man want to get (**a few**, a little) notebooks.

Lesson 8　부사

A. 밑줄 친 부사가 꾸며주는 것을 찾으세요.

1. The doctor talks <u>very</u> **fast**.
2. <u>Unfortunately</u>, **he was absent**.
3. He is **old** <u>enough</u> to take a trip by himself.
4. I **slept** <u>deeply</u> yesterday.
5. My son **learns** language <u>quickly</u>.

B. 주어진 부사(구)를 문장에 알맞게 써 넣으세요.

1. She **usually** gets up early in the morning.
2. He is rich **enough** to buy the car.
3. Tom can speak English **well**.
4. I used to go shipping with my husband **all the time**.
5. I am **really** happy to meet you.

C. 밑줄 친 단어의 뜻을 쓰세요.

1. The bus arrived ten minutes <u>late</u>.   (늦게)
2. I haven't seen him <u>lately</u>.   (최근에)
3. The man is working <u>hard</u>.   (열심히)
4. He <u>hardly</u> ever go to church.   (거의 ~ 않다)
5. The cat can jump <u>high</u>.   (높이)
6. It is a <u>highly</u> interesting movie.   (상당히)

Lesson 9   접속사/ 전치사

접속사

A. 문장에서 접속사가 연결하고 있는 것에 밑줄 치세요.

1. I want to buy <u>apples</u> and <u>tomatoes</u> at the shop.
2. We should <u>take this bus</u> or <u>wait for next one</u>.
3. <u>Tom lost his wallet</u>, but <u>his wife found it at the park</u>.
4. <u>To be</u> or <u>not to be</u>, that is a question.

B. 빈칸에 알맞은 단어를 써 넣으세요.

1. (**Both**) she (**and**) I were satisfied with the result.
2. (**Either**) John or Jane will be a first player.

C. 접속사가 이끄는 절에 밑줄을 치세요.

1. He told me that <u>he couldn't take the position</u>.
2. My wife asked if <u>I wanted to have lunch at home</u>.
3. Mike thought that <u>I had made a mistake</u>.
4. I wonder weather <u>Linda told a lie</u>.
5. That <u>she is honest</u> is clear.

전치사

A. 문장에서 전치사와 한 묶음이 되는 것에 밑줄을 치세요.

1. The USB <u>in the box</u> is expensive.
2. She went <u>to the post office</u>.
3. They usually play soccer <u>at the school</u>.
4. I haven't seen my son <u>in one year</u>.

B. 빈 칸에 알맞은 전치사를 써 넣으세요.

1. I don't have a pen to write (**with**).
2. Candy is (**from**) Austria

3. He will meet me (**on**) Sunday.

4. I will be back (**in**) five o'clock.

5. There are a lot of books (**on**) the desk.

6. The police station is (**at**) the corner of the street.

7. The chair is made (**of**) wood.

Lesson 10　부정사

A. 아래 문장에서 부정사를 확인하고, 그 용법(명사, 형용사, 부사)을 표시하세요.

1. <u>To see</u> is very important in life.　　　　　(명사)
2. I don't have time <u>to read</u> the book.　　　(형용사)
3. He wants <u>to have</u> lunch with him.　　　　(명사)
4. I don't know wat <u>to do</u>.　　　　　　　　(명사)
5. We have to do our best <u>to win</u> the game.　(부사)
6. I am glad <u>to see</u> you again.　　　　　　(부사)

B. 각 문장에서 밑줄 친 부정사의 의미상의 주어를 확인하세요.

1. <u>Tom</u> wanted <u>to see</u> me yesterday.
2. It is very kind of **you** <u>to say</u> so.
3. It is very hard for **him** <u>to get up</u> early in the morning.
4. They told <u>me</u> **to meet** you here.
5. The man stepped aside for **the lady** <u>to pass</u>.

C. 문장에 알맞은 것을 고르세요.

1. I saw him (to enter, **enter**) the classroom.
2. It is impossible (**for me**, of me) to swim in the river.
3. Jane had him (to finish, **finish**) the computer game.
4. Let me (**look at**, to look at) the bag.
5. Do you know what (do, **to do**) next?

Lesson 11   동명사

A. 아래 문장에서 동명사를 확인하고, 그 역할(주어, 보어, 목적어)을 표시하세요.

1. <u>Talking</u> with him is very interesting.   (주어)
2. The students often avoid <u>**answering**</u> their teacher's questions.   (목적어)
3. My mother stopped me from <u>**making**</u> a mistake.   (목적어)
4. Her hobby is <u>gardening</u>.   (보어)
5. Thanks for <u>**inviting**</u> me.   (목적어)

B. 아래 문장에서 알맞은 것을 선택하세요.

1. He decided (<u>**to buy**</u>, buying) the car.
2. All of them don't want (<u>**to play**</u>, playing) soccer.
3. I don't mind (to study, <u>**studying**</u>) with him.
4. My brother is busy (to do, <u>**doing**</u>) his project.
5. We can't help (to laugh, <u>**laughing**</u>) at his jokes.
6. He promised (<u>**to let**</u>, letting) me know what the teacher said.
7. Could you show me a (to sleep, <u>**sleeping**</u>) bag?

Lesson 12   분사

A. 밑줄 분사가 수식하고 있는 것을 확인하세요.

1. The **old man** <u>sitting</u> on the bench looks tired.
2. The <u>broken</u> **computer** will be fixed.
3. I couldn't believe the <u>shocking</u> **news**.
4. All of the <u>invited</u> **students** enjoyed the show.
5. The **meeting** <u>scheduled</u> for this evening is canceled.

B. 문장에 알맞은 형태를 고르세요.

1. She left the door (unlocking, **unlocked**).
2. The (retiring, **retired**) man visited the company.
3. They found the (losing, **lost**) child in the park.
4. The game was very (**exciting**, excited).
5. The building (painting, **painted**) green is a shopping center.

C. 밑줄 친 분사를 풀어쓰세요.

1. <u>Seeing</u> me, he ran away.
   When he saw ~,
2. <u>Finishing</u> the homework, she takes a nap.
   After she finished ~,
3. <u>Being</u> sick, Tom didn't attend the meeting.
   Because he was sick,
4. <u>Following</u> this road, you will find the police station.
   If you follow ~,
5. <u>Being</u> sick, I finished the project.
   Though he was sick,

Lesson 13   수동태

A.아래 문장이 능동태문장인지, 수동태 문장인지 확인하세요.

1. Tom bought Jane a ring.   (능동태)
2. The shopping mall will be opened soon.   (수동태)
3. He has waited his children for two hours.   (능동태)
4. Many students has respected the teacher.   (능동태)
5. The book was published.   (수동태)

B. 아래 문장을 수동태로 바꾸세요.

1. They broke the window yesterday.
   → The window was broken by them yesterday.
2. Shakespeare wrote Hamlet.
   → Hamlet was written by Shakespeare.
3. The policeman arrested the thief.
   → The thief was arrested by the policeman.
4. I will finish the project.
   → The project will be finished by me.
5. He gave me a gift.
   → I was given a gift by him.

C. 빈 칸에 알맞은 전치사를 쓰세요.

1. I am interested (in) English.
2. My father satisfied (with) his work.
3. The ground is covered (with) snow.
4. He was surprised (at) the news.

Lesson 14   관계사

A. 아래 문장에서 관계사와 선행사에 밑줄을 치세요.

1. I know <u>him</u> <u>who</u> lives in Denver.
2. This is <u>the phone</u> <u>which</u> I bought yesterday.
3. He met <u>a man</u> <u>whose</u> son is a singer.
4. This is the only <u>pen</u> <u>that</u> I have.
5. I don't know <u>the time</u> <u>when</u> the shop is open.

B. 두 개의 문장을 하나로 합치세요.

1. This is the book. I want to buy it.
→ **This is the book which I want to buy.**
2. This is the town. I was born there.
→ **This is the town where I was born.**
3. I bought a phone. Its screen is wide.
→ **I bought a phone whose screen is wide.**
4. He likes the computer. His father bought him it.
→ **He likes the computer which his father bought him.**
5. I know a man. He works for the company.
→ **I know a man who works for the company.**

C. 빈칸에 알맞은 관계사를 써 넣으세요.

1. Do you know the man (**who**) is watching the game?
2. I have a girl friend (**her**) father is a professor.
3. I gave my son all the money (**that/which**) I had.
4. Sunday is the day (**when**) we go to church.
5. Do you know the reason (**why**) he is so happy?

Lesson 15   일치

A. 문장에 알맞은 형태를 고르세요.

1. The pen on the desk (**is**, are) mine.

2. Tom and Bill (live, **lives**) together in the house.

3. Many a solder (**was**, were) killed at the war.

4. There (is, **are**) many people at the room.

5. Either you or I (**am**, are) supposed to attend the meeting.

6. My family (is, **are**) all very well.

7. Every boy and girl in the room (watch, **watches**) TV.

8. The doctor and artist (**is**, are) my friend.

9. Each of them (**is**, are) happy.

10. Mathematics (**is**, are) my favorite subject.

11. Not only she but also I (**like**, likes) the teacher.

12. Ten dollars (**is**, are) is too much to pay.